PORTRAITS
of
GRACE

For God is love I John 4:8b

Janet Sherrard

PORTRAITS
of
GRACE

Janet Sherrard
with Stephanie Judd

Xulon Press
555 Winderley Pl, Suite 225
Maitland, FL 32751
407.339.4217
www.xulonpress.com

© 2024 by Janet Sherrard

Contribution by Stephanie Judd

All rights reserved solely by the author. The author guarantees all contents are original and do not infringe upon the legal rights of any other person or work. No part of this book may be reproduced in any form without the permission of the author.

Due to the changing nature of the Internet, if there are any web addresses, links, or URLs included in this manuscript, these may have been altered and may no longer be accessible. The views and opinions shared in this book belong solely to the author and do not necessarily reflect those of the publisher. The publisher therefore disclaims responsibility for the views or opinions expressed within the work.

Unless otherwise indicated, Scripture quotations taken from the King James Version (KJV) – *public domain*.

Paperback ISBN-13: 979-8-86850-155-5
Ebook ISBN-13: 979-8-86850-156-2

DEDICATION

Portraits of Grace is dedicated to the memories of all those whom God
has used to teach me about His deep love and everlasting mercy.
Most of all to Jesus, the Author and Finisher of our faith
The one who transforms difficult, even impossible situations,
and creates a beautiful tapestry of His mercy and grace;
for our good and His glory.

EPIGRAPH

"I will remember the works of the Lord, surely I will remember thy wonders of old" (Psalm 77;11).

"Now also when I am gray-headed, O God, forsake me not: until I have shewed thy strength unto this generation, and thy power to every one that is to come" (Psalm 71:18).

TABLE OF CONTENTS

Chapter 1	The Redemption	1
Chapter 2	The Call	7
Chapter 3	The God Who Intercedes	11
Chapter 4	Fruit from the Flats	17
Chapter 5	The Anchor	21
Chapter 6	Memories From the Husband	27
Chapter 7	The Watch	33
Chapter 8	The Surrender	37
Chapter 9	The Atheist	41
Chapter 10	Reach for Jesus	45
Chapter 11	The Wordless Witness	49
Chapter 12	Precious in His Sight	53
Chapter 13	The Divine Detour	57
Chapter 14	Not about Hypocrisy	61
Chapter 15	The Anointing	65
Chapter 16	The Big Question	69

Chapter 17	Molasses Cookies	73
Chapter 18	The Final Gift	77
Chapter 19	The Painting	81
Chapter 20	One Special Night	85
Chapter 21	Hope Redefined	87
Chapter 22	The Challenge	93
Chapter 23	The Blood	97
Chapter 24	The Vision	101
Chapter 25	One More Bowl of Cornflakes	105
Chapter 26	The Escape	109
Chapter 27	The Lily	113
Chapter 28	The Bible and the Bear	117
Chapter 29	The Grateful Heart	121
Chapter 30	The Example	125
Conclusion	The Stewardship of Grief and Pain	129

INTRODUCTION

What an awesomely beautiful day it is! To have the day off to rest and relax, indeed, makes it a blessed day. Just lie under a tree and watch the clouds traverse the sky and feel the soft breeze whisper "all is well." Thank you, God, for the beauty in the world and Your peace in my heart. You are worthy of all my praise and worship!

Smoke fills the sky as fast as the blast interrupts the peace! Bright red-hot flames shoot hungrily for the yellow leaves on the trees. Sparks ignite the dry leaves on the ground and race to devour anything that will burn. The beautiful day disintegrates in an instant!

An evening rain cools the hot coals. All the precious treasures, the memories, and the ordinary necessities of living; reduced to ashes in a matter of moments.

Slowly, pensively, and cautiously rummage through the rubbish. Sinking hope sheds a tear of remorse. It happened so fast. Nothing left. Only what one can remember of things never to be held in hand again.

There is nothing but ash where the cornerstone once proudly stood. Sift through it anyway, aimlessly. What is that? Something firm! Brush the dust off. It is the size of a brick. It is a brick, a brick of gold! The hidden treasure of gold would not burn.

Amidst the loss and ashes of grief and pain, a treasure lies. Somewhere, not easy to find, yet as sure and solid as that brick of gold, the grace of God waits to be discovered. Seek for that 'pearl of great price' hiding in the darkness. Every dark and hard place can yield a *Portrait of Grace*, God's amazing grace, for those with eyes to see.

Grief and pain are common denominators of human life. There is "a time to weep and a time to laugh; a time to mourn and a time to dance" (Ecclesiastes 3:4). When we have no sense of God's presence, and we cannot see His smile; when the nearest and dearest to our heart is stripped away from us, let us pray: "Lord, help me to love You in the dark. Help me to be faithful when nothing encourages my faith. Jesus, use me, teach me, hold me in my distress. Make me a faithful steward when it seems I have nothing in my hand. Help me see the 'gold brick' of grief and pain as a precious seed in Your hands; that I may trust you enough to surrender my circumstances to Your sovereignty."

> "He that goeth forth and weepeth, bearing precious seed, shall doubtless come again with rejoicing, bringing his sheaves with him (Psalm 126:6).

> "The sorrows of death compassed me, and the pains of hell got hold upon me: I found trouble and sorrow. Then I called upon the name of the Lord; O Lord, I beseech thee, deliver my soul. Gracious is the Lord, and righteous; yea, our God is merciful. The Lord preserveth the simple: I was brought low, and He helped me. Return unto thy rest, O my soul; for the Lord hath dealt bountifully with thee" (Psalm 116:3-7).

Chapter 1
THE REDEMPTION

"Go out into the highways and hedges and compel them to come in" (Luke 14:23 KJV).

"I wish that old woman would just get in her rocking chair and rock and leave me alone!"

I slammed down the phone with heated emotion. My dad was in the room, and I was hoping to score a few brownie points for my anti-god and anti-church attitude; the very same attitude he had displayed so well during my fifteen years, but I had forgotten a crucial point.

"You were disrespectful to your elders!" His voice resonated with anger and disgust. He informed me with no uncertainty, "You will go to that church next Sunday!"

How could I have been so stupid? He always had the last word. I braced myself for the shame and embarrassment that undoubtedly would befall me. I had made a grave error and I had to fix it.

Fueled with anger, both at myself for being so stupid and at the rejection from my dad, I created Plan B: I would go to that church on Sunday, listen intently, scrutinize everyone closely, and find as many inconsistencies and fabrications as possible. Upon my return home, I would give a carefully worded yet 'respectful' report. His assumptions about the church and Christianity would be confirmed and I would be vindicated. Or so I thought.

Meanwhile, God had Plan C...

That wintery Sunday morning dawned bright and clear. Filled with dread, my feet were unusually heavy, and it was not just the weight of my winter boots. I walked six blocks to the church. This old woman had been hounding me for months, ever since the church began canvasing my neighborhood and learned of my meager existence. She was always calling me or stopping by to invite me to one event or another. Worse yet, my dad, of all things, was forcing me to go to church! He was the one person I was sure would be in my corner about this church thing. I had truly blown it.

As I neared the church, my rebellious nature reared its ugly head. To ensure my Plan B was etched firmly in my mind, I increased my resolve and determination. Taking a deep breath, I reached out and pulled the door open. Onslaught! A gang of teenagers I had never met engulfed me with hugs and greetings!

In all the commotion, my rebellion and Plan B got lost. For the life of me, I could not find them. Swept along in the current of teens, I found myself adrift in a classroom. Uncertain of all that was happening, my ears perked up at the mention of history. The class was about history. I loved history! The fact that it turned out to be Christian history did not quench my curiosity. All my defenses and resolves disappeared.

Unfortunately, the church service still found me entangled with all those teens, and in the front row no less! No room for an escape or a quick exit. I was completely disarmed and defenseless. Words and music began to fog my mind. I failed again.

My carefully devised Plan B was long gone, never to return. Thankfully, no one asked me any questions on my return home. Perhaps I could just forget that this whole thing ever happened-or so I hoped.

Monday morning dawned; I was back at school. Today was gym class. I hated gym class, especially swimming. I had never been around a body of water larger than a bathtub. It scared me.

"Today, we will learn how to dive," the teacher announced. Fear pierced the very core of my being with its' sharpest arrows. I began to panic. *I can't do this*! Inwardly screaming, I frantically searched for an escape route.

The Redemption

Finding none, I crouched on the side of the pool, hoping against all hope that I could somehow go unnoticed.

Suddenly, someone pushed my back. Chlorinated water rushed to fill my gaping mouth. Frantically, I opened my mouth, gasping for air, only to be greeted by more water. Sheer terror gripped me! All I could think was, *I can't breathe; I can't breathe; I'm drowning!*

All my fears were confirmed in an instant. The bottom of that nine-foot pool came rushing at me. Darkness closed in around me. A volcanic eruption of emotions spewed forth; flashing its ugly memories of jealousy, hatred, anger, strife, and pride, followed by arrogance and deception.

Simultaneously, a radiant light beamed its' dagger into my heart, *there really is a God and I am going to have to give an account of my life to Him!* Trepidation seized my heart with that last thought. I was filled with terror, certain I was going to succumb to a watery grave, when two strong arms locked underneath my own arms, and my head rose to the surface. As they laid me prostrate on the pool deck and pumped my arms to remove the water from my lungs, my mind changed direction as rapidly as my body had been delivered from the deep.

Gasping for air to replace the water in my lungs and struggling with the harsh cough, gratitude began to fill my soul. I was not dying. I had another chance. I determined to take this proffered olive branch and seek after God.

God's Plan C: Operation Conviction.
God's Execution: Triumphant!

No one had to force me to go to church now. I snuck out of the house to attend for fear of being denied the opportunity. Every time the doors were open, I was there, desperate to know what to do about the darkness in my soul. I did not want to face God with whatever it was. I learned the word sin. I asked questions, studied, and sought relief from my heavy burden.

PORTRAITS OF GRACE

The gap in my understanding was finally bridged on a Sunday evening. For the first time, I understood God's whole plan. I was a sinner. I identified with Romans 3:23 ,"For all have sinned and come short of the glory of God." My near demise left no question in my mind, I was a sinner, and an unbelievably bad one at that! The penalty I knew quite well. "For the wages of sin is death, but the gift of God is eternal life through Jesus Christ our Lord" (Romans 6:23). Boy, did I ever get that! I had been on my way to a watery grave. It was then I clearly saw the mercy I so desperately sought, the forgiveness my heart yearned for.

> "For God so loved the world, that He gave His only begotten Son that whosoever believeth in Him should not perish but have everlasting life" (John 3:16).

I was included in that "whosoever."

> "But God commended His love toward us, in that while we were yet sinners, Christ died for us" (Romans 5:8).

Christ died for me! How could He love a sinner such as I? He loved me when I was drowning! He loves me now!

Then the promise of "That if thou shalt confess with thy mouth the Lord Jesus, and shalt believe in thine heart that God hath raised Him from the dead, thou shalt be saved" (Romans 10:9). He promised!

The congregation rose to sing an invitational hymn. My heart ached for this salvation, but I found my feet shackled to the floor. I could not move them! There were so many people, and I was afraid of them... Verse after verse, they sang. All the while the battle raged within my heart. I longed to step out, yet I was afraid to. I could scarcely bear my longing for this free gift, but my feet were frozen!

After what must have been the eighth verse, the preacher pleaded with the congregation for patience as he said, "There is one more soul that needs to come." I knew that soul was mine.

This was my last chance, but I could not move! At that point, the blessed Holy Spirit whispered to my soul, "If you'll take one step for Me, I will go the rest of the way with you."

Hope sprung up in my heart. I can do one step. I took one step! My only memory after that first step found me crumpled at the foot of the cross pleading for forgiveness, my face awash with tears of remorse.

That night my precious Savior washed me whiter than snow by the power of His shed blood, my sin to be remembered against me no more!

God's Plan C: Operation Conversion
Execution: Triumphant

Chapter 2
THE CALL

"Who hath saved us, and called us with a holy calling, not according to our works, but according to His own purpose and grace, which was given us in Christ Jesus before the world began" (II Timothy 1:9).

"Can you help me with the book cart this afternoon?" Linda asked as the school bus rumbled up to speed. "Sherry usually does, but she is sick today."

"I guess so; I've never done it before." I replied, half-heartedly, wondering why I was the one chosen out of all the girls on the bus.

"That's okay. We just get books from the hospital library. We choose things like colorful magazines, short stories, or picture books for people to look at while they are recuperating. As we wheel the cart down the hospital hallways, we ask the patients in each room if they would like to borrow anything. Then we write down who borrowed what. To make it simple, you just offer the books, and I will keep the record on the ledger."

The school bus pulled up near the hospital and we got off. I had never been in a hospital before, at least not since I was born. I trailed along behind Linda, my head turning at all the sights, sounds and smells that caught my attention. Linda continued chatting, oblivious to the fact I was totally awed. We soon arrived at a room marked 'volunteers.'

"I'm called a candy-striper," she explained tossing me an identical red and white striped apron to wear. "I think it's because these aprons make us look like candy canes." *OK, I thought, so it is Christmas in May.*

Linda pushed the cart down the halls as I poked my head in each room and asked if anyone wanted something to read or look at. Linda's plan worked well. One hour later we were in the last hall just before finishing our task.

Then, it happened. As I poked my head in a room, a frail, crippled old lady struggled to raise her head off her pillow. "Help me, help me!" she pleaded. Her frantic plea tugged at my heartstrings. But, alas, I had not a clue what to do or even say to her.

A Voice spoke within me; that still, small Voice, the same Voice that had encouraged me six weeks earlier to take that 'first step' towards Jesus. No one else could hear the voice, but I would know it anywhere since becoming one of His 'sheep'.

"This is what I want you to do." It was Him, the Blessed Holy Spirit. True to His Word, He was walking the rest of the way with me. The next step was clear. All through the night I pondered the implications of the sudden encounter. Was Jesus honestly calling me to be a nurse? How could this be? I did not have a clue about healthcare, let alone an interest in medicine. *I'm not even a good student*, I mused to myself in the privacy of my room. *I have always taken the easiest classes and I cannot afford to go to college.* Heavier and heavier the call weighed. The longer I pondered it, the more hindrances, and outright obstacles, defeated me. Nonetheless, if it was what Jesus wanted....

My school counselor cautioned, "This is quite a change for you as you only have two years of high school left. Nursing requires a lot of science and mathematics courses." She looked over my school record and compared it to her list of known requirements from nursing schools in the area. I needed a lot more science classes! I had no interest in science. The only thing worse than all that science was the math credits!

"You will have to take Advanced Biology next year. Then in your senior year you will have to take Physics and Chemistry." She continued thumbing through the requirements as my heart tightened in my throat. "Oh, I see you will also need to take Geometry and Algebra II next year."

She looked above her half-rimmed glasses, awaiting my decision. It was the end of May, meaning I needed to make my decision soon. The deadline to sign up for next year's classes was only a week away!

Alone with my Bible in my room that night, the call remained firm. But could I have been mistaken? Could this just be an emotional reaction? Such a heavy load of courses doomed me to failure. If I failed, I would not be a nurse anyway. So why even try?

"Lord, confirm to me what I am to do." I pleaded as tears brought release to my troubled spirit.

His Word addressed my valid concerns, "Faithful is He that calleth you who also will do it" (I Thessalonians 5:24),

"Study to show thyself approved unto God, a workman that needeth not to be ashamed, rightly dividing the word of truth" (II Timothy 2:15).

That next Sunday, a missionary nurse spoke to my Sunday school class. Millions had never heard of Jesus. Souls all over the world were lost in the darkness from which I had so recently been delivered. She told stories of how God used her nursing skills, not only to deliver people from their physical pain, but also to point them to Jesus who could deliver them from the spiritual bondage of sin.

"If you are not a soul-winner at home, in your own culture and your own language, you will not be a soul-winner in a foreign culture and a foreign language," she cautioned.

I needed to be a soul winner. I needed to be wise. This was the rest of the call.

The nurse challenged our class with Proverbs 11:30, "He that winneth souls is wise."

Monday morning found me again in the counselors' office, this time to sign up in obedience to the call; oblivious to all the twists and turns on which this journey would take me.

> "Commit thy way unto the Lord, trust also in Him; and He shall bring it to pass" (Psalm 37:5).

Chapter 3
The God Who Intervenes

"For the battle is not yours, but God's" (I Chronicles 20:15b).

"One-third of this freshman class will not be here to start the second semester." Such was the matter-of-fact welcome to the first-year class of the diploma nursing school. "We can't waste time or space on you if you are not dedicated to becoming a nurse. If you graduate from this school, your training will be recognized as top-of-the-line, and you can get a job anywhere," continued the Matron of Nurses.

One hundred and twenty potential nurses just received a blow to the gut. Would it be the girl on either side of me or would it be me that would be axed from the program? We all silently wondered the same thing. Our excited bubble about this new chapter in our lives had just popped!

Twenty-one credit hours the first semester kept us in a class or in a clinical situation from 7 am to 5 pm daily. Less disciplined students were curbed from exiting the building by the curfew, placed on our probationary status, which started promptly at 6 pm on Sunday and continued through Thursday evening. I thought my classmates must be much smarter and more experienced than I for they found time to watch television and visit from room to room while I struggled to digest the massive servings of vital information. I lacked discernment to separate the critical information from the interesting non-essentials. Insecurity drove me to fear free time. I had to focus. I had a call. I could not fail..

Hidden from my view, God had another curriculum for me. His design was to develop trust, prayer, wisdom, and control of my tongue. Always residing in my heart, the Comforter abided as my guide and encourager.

Thankfully, God had supplied a job for me during my senior year of high school which not only provided funds for the first year of school, but also forced me to learn time management skills and to prioritize my tasks. *One out of every three students will not return in January.* I could not get that out of my head. So, my Comforter served as my guide to be aware of forces and opportunities which could distract me or even worse, completely derail me from this journey.

Many of the prerequisite first semester classes were contracted by the nursing school to the local junior college. One of those classes had a pot-hole in it for me. I had diligently prepared for the mid-term exam. The ten-question test only asked for the author of each assigned research paper. I could have recited the main points of each article and even answered essay questions, however, I did not know even one author. I failed it. That really upset me. If something gets under my skin deep enough it finds my tongue. Up went my hand.

"If you are in a bad accident and I am your nurse in the emergency room, what do you want me to know, the name of the authors of my medical books or what is in the books?" That smart remark earned me a smarting "F" for my mid-term grade.

> "Set a watch, O Lord, before my mouth; Keep the door of my lips" (Psalm 141:3).

A week later, the mid-term probation status was posted outside the mail-room door. In alphabetical order my name was listed with the forty+ students deemed most likely to fail. I raced to my secret place of prayer. I bounded up to the top of the dormitory stairs and collapsed in a heap at the service entrance to the roof. No words could express the heaviness and ache in my heart, however, my Comforter interpreted to the Father what I could not even verbalize. Then my Comforter encouraged me to take the matter to the Matron of Nurses.

Trembling, I waited for her at the scheduled time. I whispered a prayer for guidance as I was escorted into her intimidating presence. When asked, I humbly presented to her what I believed was the reason for the resounding "F."

"Why do you want off probation?" she asked, her face expressionless.

"That I might attend church on Sunday and Wednesday evenings." I responded meekly.

"Your reputation has reached my ears before this meeting. You do not party or participate in questionable activities. You are studious and have an 'A' average in all your other classes. Your probation is canceled." Just as matter of factly, she exited the room.

> *"Be careful for nothing, but in everything by prayer and supplication with thanksgiving let your requests be made known unto God" (Philippians 4:6).*

That it might be all of God

In the spring of my freshman year, my classmates decided I should have a social life. If not by choice, then they would make it by force. Six of them pinned me to the floor in preparation to execute their plan. Desperate to escape what I knew would be an ungodly destination, I mentally shot a prayer. God gave me sudden strength enabling me to break free. I raced for the stairwell. My surprised captors raced in hot pursuit. Bounding two steps at a time, I purposely opened the door to every floor as I flew by to confuse them.

Onward I sped, above the sixth floor to the stairs that lead to the roof. There, crouched in my place of prayer, quietly I thanked God as I heard my would-be captors searching from floor to floor, baffled by my escape. God had provided the way of escape. Never again was such an attempt made. From that time on, I was nick-named "Mama Bear." For the rest of my time in school, my classmates sought me out for counsel, tutoring and emotional and spiritual support on our long, hard journey to become nurses.

> "Be strong in the Lord and in the power of His might" (Ephesians 6:10).

That it might be all of God

The second year of training presented yet another hurdle; the administering of intramuscular injections; in layperson terms, I had to give shots. I was terrified of needles myself and even more terrified of using a victim as a dart board. We practiced injections on an orange. That was safe enough. But whenever an opportunity to practice on a human arose, I held back. I hoped against hope to become invisible. Alas, my selective avoidance caught up with me. I was the lone holdout and could no longer hide.

My victim was a skin and bones edition of the living dead. He was crying with pain. I had not anticipated how much easier my needle would penetrate human skin than it did an orange. The needle bounded off his hip bone, terrifying me. I screamed inwardly, biting my lip to prevent the escape of sound from frightening my victim. *Lord, Help me!* As I pushed the plunger on the syringe his skin correspondingly filled like a balloon. Shocked at the unexpected lump, I finished the task, still screaming on the inside. Fellow students and my instructor who had observed this traumatic event, followed my hasty departure from the scene to the break room.

Completely wiped out, I broke down in uncontrollable sobbing. Unaware of those around me I gave voice to my pain. "Lord, I can't do it! I just can't do it! I'll never be a nurse!" My will to obey God's plan drained completely from the hole in my defeated heart. There, in my weakest moment, my Comforter again appeared.

"My grace is sufficient for thee, for my strength is made perfect in weakness" (II Corinthians 12:9).

That it might be all of God

My final rotation before graduation was psychiatry. Overwhelmed with the inhumane treatment of souls facing traumatic and difficult life situations, my mind could not find any logic in the methods or hypothesis employed to treat 'mental illness'. Clients were turned into zombies by electric shock treatments, drugs, drugs, and more drugs. Moreover, scenes from challenging times in my childhood further crippled my mind. The theories did not make sense.

A week before graduation I was called to meet with the administrative team of the nursing school. I failed the class. I could only pray, "If it is still Your will for me to be a nurse, You will have to do it, Lord." The team questioned me, reviewed the rest of my school record and my character values. Thankfully, God had held me steady through those three years and I had stood as an example of the believers, albeit-not always the smartest!

The final decision came. "You have excelled in all other areas of nursing. This appears to be a personal issue for you. If you promise not to try to be a psychiatric nurse, you can graduate. If you can pass the state boards for nursing, you will be a nurse."

Those conditions were not hard to agree with. God helped me and I did pass the boards, even the section on psychiatry, with flying colors.

"Being confident of this very thing, that He that has begun a good work in you will perform it until the day of Jesus Christ" (Philippians 1:6).

That it might be all of God

Chapter 4
Fruit from the Flats

"Suffer (let) the little children to come unto me and forbid them not for of such is the kingdom of God" (Luke 18:16).

"But why did he have to die?" cried little Timmy, his towhead buried in his hands. It was Easter Sunday and Timmy had only been coming to church for about a month.

"Jesus loved us so much; He did not want us to have to die for our sins. Jesus took our punishment so we would not have to," I explained. I prayed God would open his eleven-year-old heart to the precious truth.

"What is sin?" I asked, opening the discussion for class participation. I acknowledged the redhead in the second row. "Yes, Mandy."

"Sin is not obeying God," she confidently asserted.

"Sin is what Adam and Eve did in the Garden of Eden," Bobby interjected. "Only one thing God told them not to do and they had to do it! Eat that Apple! Now we all have sin. We are born with that awful sinful nature."

"You are both right." I affirmed them. "What is the first thing you want to do when told to do something or not to do something?" I asked.

Several classmates giggled. "We do the opposite!" they laughed.

"Again, you are right!" I exclaimed. "That's what all of us do because of sin in our hearts. God sent His perfect Son, Jesus, to come to earth as a baby. Jesus grew up and never did anything wrong. He obeyed his parents. He loved everyone. When He grew up, He spent three years teaching people about His Father. He healed the sick and raised the dead. He forgave sin. He could do all that because He was God." Every eye was watching me intently.

"Jesus came to earth for a purpose. He loved us so much He came to take the punishment for our sin. He wanted us to live in Heaven with Him forever when we die. When Adam and Eve sinned, death came into the world as punishment for sin. Only someone that did not have sin could take our punishment. That someone was Jesus. Jesus willingly went to the cross to be crucified; a painful death. He was buried for three days. Then He rose from the dead. He defeated death! Now, if we confess our sins and ask Him to forgive our sins, He is waiting with open arms to love us, and take us to heaven to be with Him forever when our earthly body dies." Timmy's furrowed brow reflected his effort to understand.

I loved this special child, his tender earnestness melted my heart. Diagnosed with Cystic Fibrosis, when he was three years old, he was of small stature. He could have been mistaken for a five- or six-year-old. His chronic cough limited his ability to do anything that required physical exertion, but nothing limited his inquisitive mind.

Timmy lived with his mom and three siblings in a housing development down in the hollow, about a mile from our inner-city church. 'The Flats' as it was called, nourished an environment of sin, sloth, depression, and forlorn hopelessness. 'Down in the hollow', the Flats were out of sight and mind for most people, who never thought about those poor souls, much less prayed for them.

Even so, God placed a call on Ida, the pastor's wife, to minister to those lost sheep. Every week she trekked down to the 'Flats,' adorned with a spirit of meekness. She spent time with the people there and built relationships with them. Though physically, congestive heart failure restricted her activity, her spiritual heart overflowed with love and compassion to reach lost souls. Christ's love flowed from her heart like a river, flowing down to the 'Flats.' Fruit from those visits began to blossom. Many ventured to come to church. Timmy and his family were among them.

On a clear Sunday morning not long after Easter, Timmy and his mom answered the Spirit's call on their hearts and bowed at the life-changing altar. There, Jesus removed the heavy burden of sin and planted a light in their hearts. Timmy's mom rejoiced and grew in the Lord, a witness to the change Jesus makes; a change made more pronounced by the environment of the 'Flats.'

Little Timmy–God had an incredibly special job for that incredibly special agent of His; it was a place of ministry. No one could do this job like Timmy could. His call was to be a missionary to the hospital. As his disease progressed, the medications and breathing treatments his mom did at home could no longer sustain him. His cough lacked the strength needed to remove the thick secretions from his damaged lungs. Repeated infections and pneumonia placed him in his pulpit in the hospital. His radiant, bubbling love for Jesus captured hearts and spread as a contagion everywhere he went.

I often worked on the pediatric floor as a nurse aide my Senior year. On that same floor, Timmy would be hospitalized for weeks at a time. His smile brightened the room. As breathing became increasingly difficult, he was placed in an oxygen tent. He rarely got home and even more rarely was he able to go to church. Still, God fed him with His manna which Timmy shared with everyone who came into his room. His overflowing love for Jesus captured unsuspecting souls. He just HAD to tell everyone about his Jesus. So sweet and kind was his love, so cheerful his disposition, that everyone loved and even longed to be in his presence.

I could not help but notice the housekeeper taking particular care to keep his room extra clean. While she worked, this child would tell her how much Jesus loved her. Though he could only speak two or three words without taking another labored breath, he assured her that she too could have the peace of God in her heart. I observed the lady from dietary linger as she slowly slipped his food tray through the slit in the oxygen tent. She listened as he declared the Bread of Life to her. Jesus said, "I am the bread of life. He that cometh to me shall never hunger; and he that believeth on me shall never thirst" (John 6:35).

The nurses were most profoundly affected. Anticipatory grief weighed our hearts down as we spent hours giving him breathing treatments and medications. Every day our assessments confirmed his failing status. We all loved him and his sweet angelic nature. He never complained or even verbalized a desire to be or do anything but what his Savior had called him to be and do.

I cared for him the day he could no longer sit up. He lacked energy to eat. Sleep wrapped him in a blanket of love. Slowly, he slipped into a coma. I held his hand through the slit in the oxygen tent. A smile broke across his sleeping face as the last breath on earth became his first breath in heaven.

> "Well done, thou good and faithful servant. Enter thou into the joy of thy Lord" (Matthew 25:21).

Chapter 5
THE ANCHOR

"....lay hold upon the hope set before us: which hope we have as an anchor of the soul" (Hebrews 6:18b-19a).

"I must have walked into the wrong church!" I told myself in stunned silence. It was 1969. I had worked a double shift Saturday night. I did not doubt in my fatigue that I could have lost my way. Stepping outside, I did a double-take on the church sign. No, I was certainly in the right spot, but something was egregiously off. With a bit of uncertainty, I made my way back inside. I was utterly stunned by the scene before me.

The once unified community of believers was divided into two distinct groups. I looked from side to side. On one side the women sported fresh haircuts and donned stunning new pant suits. Glistening wedding rings encircled their ring fingers to complete their ensemble. From the gleaming smiles on their faces, it was clear they enjoyed their liberation from the imposing dress standards previously expected of them. I scarcely recognized them.

On the other side of the church my eyes spotted a small band who held fast to our traditional simplicity. I had strived to show honor and obedience to God by gladly embracing all the external appearances anyone told me would please God. How could so many renounce God's grace in such a short time? What could cause my dear brothers and sisters in Christ to abandon the safe ship of simplicity? My spiritual family of the last two years was now divided; both in appearance and in opinion. What had caused such

PORTRAITS OF GRACE

an abrupt change? I felt my spiritual anchor begin to shift as I was tossed to and fro by waves of shock and confusion.

The annual church camp meeting and conference was held the first week of August. I was not in attendance as I worked at the hospital that summer between my Junior and Senior year. Therefore, I did not know the momentous decision church leaders agreed on during that conference. I did not know they voted to update our standards of external appearance. I did not know the majority viewed our simplicity as a stumbling block to the world around us. I never dreamed our simplicity and our traditions could be considered anything but what I perceived them to be; an outward symbol of an inward work, a lifestyle that honored God and reflected His love to a lost world. Just one vote dissolved our simplistic, visual symbol of separation from the world. The remnant of church members remained steadfast. They struggled and prayed for their fellow believers who had embraced this new form of legalized freedom.

Devastated, I yearned to 'fix' it. I felt like my parents were divorcing. The church (my mother) was divorcing God (my Father). Fellowship with my Christian family became strained as the tug of war pressed me to choose sides. The liberated side set their anchor in Matthew 7:1, "Judge not that ye be not judged." The remnant anchored to II Thessalonians 2:15, "Therefore brethren, stand fast and hold the traditions which ye have been taught." Neither side appeared to be heeding Paul's admonition in Philippians 1:9-10, "And this I pray that your love may abound yet more and more in knowledge and in all judgment; that ye may approve things that are excellent; that ye may be sincere and without offence till the day of Christ."

I no longer knew what was the right or wrong way to live. The only thing I knew for sure was that Jesus loved me. He changed my life. I couldn't turn back. Jesus was too precious to me. However, I could not go on. This new way of doing the "Christian life" hurled me into a state of confusion and spiritual distress. I hungered for the old ways. My church family taught me those ways. Those ways provided comfort, stability, and sweet fellowship with Jesus. The storm's dark clouds of confusion, disorientation, disillusionment, and skepticism rolled in. Sadly, I discovered my anchor dragged in shifting sand.

Independent church groups sprang up. They claimed to hold fast to the ways of our forefathers. Adrift on troubled waters, I set my eye on what appeared to be a lighthouse on the distant shore. Arriving late to one of those conservative camp meetings, I pulled my new, brown 1971 Dodge Dart into the only vacant parking space; front and center behind the tabernacle. Seemingly inspired by my car, the message focused on the sin of owning a new car, the vanity of sporty steering wheels, and the lust of life tied up in hubcaps.

At the end of the service a denouncing altar call did nothing to penetrate my hardening heart. Astonishingly, a young lady about my age approached the altar, sobbing, amidst a barrage of denunciations from the pulpit. The evangelist boomed accusingly at her, "What are you doing here? You know you do not mean business with God!" Revolted, I ran to my wicked, sinful Dodge Dart, and spit dirt in the air as I sped away, praying for that poor victim of spiritual abuse. The independent church movement debunked. The lighthouse: only a mirage on the horizon. I needed an anchor.

My former pastor recommended that I enroll in a particular conservative Bible college. One month before the term began, I became ill with a mysterious disease. A fever of 106 degrees cost me most of my waist-long hair. The rest of my hair was damaged and brittle. I was shunned as soon as I arrived on campus. Unknown to me, it was a sin for women to wear their hair down. That's what prostitutes did. As my hair was only shoulder length, I was judged as having cut my hair, also, a sin.

Chapel services served only to bring more confusion and spiritual distress. An evening chapel message challenged us to do what we could for God now, because in six months America would be overthrown by Russia and we would no longer be free. In despair, I asked the Dean of Women for permission for late lights to read my Bible. Denied. I asked to read in the main sitting area so that she might see what I was doing. Denied. Disillusioned and dejected, I returned to my room, entered my closet, prayed, and quoted all the scripture I could remember. *How is this different than what it will be in a prison camp?* I asked myself. Guided only by moonlight, I packed my belongings into my car. Lights off, I drove away at 3 a.m. I needed an anchor.

The first Sunday back in my 'home church' the new pastor greeted me with, "You are out of God's will because you left Bible College." He knew nothing of what had happened. I left the church.

All my efforts to find a place of refuge, fellowship, and most importantly, God's will and the sense of His presence, came crashing down. I felt my purpose in life had been snatched by a violent, angry sea. I floundered in a dark and desolate place. Fighting to keep my head above the raging waves of depression, I pleaded, "Lord, where are You? Where is Your truth? Help me as You did so many times in the past. I need your presence. I need your peace. I need you, Lord!" I needed an anchor.

> "And ye shall seek me and find me when ye shall search for me with all your heart" (Jeremiah 29:13).

The next Sunday morning, the little white country church near where I grew up, flashed across my mind. It was February. The roads were clear. Maybe this was God telling me where to go. When I arrived a bit late, many welcomed me with warm greetings. Hearty voices worshiped in song and warmed the chilly bands of fear wrapped around my heart.

The Sunday School lesson featured Adam and Eve's expulsion from the Garden of Eden. God created this beautiful garden and placed His crowning creation, man, in it to enjoy and care for it. God loved to walk with His children in the cool of the evening through that perfect environment. Because God wanted them to love and serve Him by choice, He gave them free will. They could choose to love and serve Him or not. Only one fruit was forbidden them of all the bounty in that beautiful garden. All was well until the Tempter(Satan) planted seeds of doubt in the minds of Adam. Sadly, they chose to question God's love for them. The consequence of that choice (sin) was physical death, as well as eternal damnation of the soul. That consequence infected the human race with the same sinful, fallen, nature. However, God's omniscient love provided a plan to redeem His cherished creation. He killed a lamb, an innocent lamb, to provide proper clothing for them as the glory of God no longer covered their nakedness. The sacrifice of that lamb foreshadowed the promised Savior who would shed His sinless blood, die and rise again to pay the penalty of death for man's sin. "And I will put enmity between thee and the woman, and between thy seed and her seed: it shall bruise thy head, and thou shalt bruise his heel" (Genesis 3:15). The seed of the woman is the first prophesy of the future Messiah.

Suddenly, I realized in my zealousness to show love for Jesus, I had failed to seek Him only. I had aligned with a culture that was fallible. When my mother, the church, fell from the standard they themselves had established, my search for truth looked for a lighthouse that resembled those same standards. Along the journey to find my anchor, the old self-righteousness of the Pharisees threatened to drown any hope of freedom in Christ and bury me in discouragement and despondency.

My Comforter drew close once more and cleansed me of the spiritual fog that had clouded my mind for two years. The truth I had been searching for all this time was in the Word. "In the beginning was the Word, and the Word was with God, and the Word was God. The same was in the beginning with God. All things were made by Him; and without Him was not anything made that was made. In Him was life; and the life was the light of men. and the light shineth in darkness; and the darkness comprehended it not (John 1:1-5).

It was still His blood that saved from sin. It was all in His Word and only His Word. I found my anchor.

> "For God is not the author of confusion, but of peace, as in all the churches of the saints" (I Corinthians 14:33).

Cherish your traditions or cast them all aside.
Just be sure in God's will, you ever shall abide.
Keep your eyes on Jesus, surrender to His will.
He has a plan just for you, you have a place to fill.

Chapter 6
Memories from the Husband

"In all thy ways acknowledge Him and He shall direct thy paths" (Proverbs 3:6).

I remember the first time I noticed her. It was at the Christmas program put on by our local country school. Although I had graduated 8th grade three years previously, my whole family still attended all events at the school. Not only was this a family tradition, it also was a community tradition. She hesitated before pulling out the piano bench as she was the last one of her second-grade class to perform. With her back to the audience, she hammered out each note of 'Jingle Bells' as deliberately as a metronome.

I had a chance to get to know her when she was thirteen. Her family was in a difficult situation and needed housing. My mother's parents had recently passed away, so my dad offered them their large, white farmhouse. The farmhouse was surrounded by one hundred acres which my dad and I farmed. Soon after they moved in, I went to check the wheat we had planted there. It was the first week of June. There she was. No longer a little schoolgirl but a little lady, at least that was how she looked to me.

I decided to put the spring hay crop in the barn behind the house. When I arrived at the farm, a wagon overflowing with bales of sweet-smelling hay in tow, she and her siblings all ran out to meet me and 'help.' Soon, the novelty of the hay wagon and the conveyor that transported the hay up into the barn mow wore off and the four younger ones wandered off. Yet, she stayed. She learned how to unload the wagon. It proved to be a help to me. I compensated her by listening to what she needed to say, while we sat, dangling our legs off the empty hay wagon. I had just turned 25 and she was 13 going on 14.

Sadly, they found a house in town and moved by the end of the next summer. I waited another 15 months but couldn't get her off my mind. I summoned up the courage to go to her house and ask her dad if I could take her to a high school basketball game.

"NO and don't ask again!" he briskly replied. Then we sat in the living room and exchanged small talk about the weather and such. All the children sat like stuffed animals perched on chairs and spoke not a word. I had no opportunity to speak to her. I could only give her a smile which she warmly returned.

A few months later a family friend informed us she had started coming to their church and gave her heart to Jesus. That was welcome news, for she had confided many difficult things to me during the time we put up hay. Not long after that, this friend shared that God had called her to be a nurse. Perhaps, that included being a missionary nurse, they thought. I knew then that I loved her. Yet, if God had a call on her life, I did not want to be a hindrance.

It happened on a cold February Sunday nine years later. I was in my usual pew two rows from the front, next to the east window of that near century-old Methodist Church. I heard the rustle of someone entering the church a few minutes late. It was her! I could hardly wait for the service to end. I hastened to welcome her. I invited her to my parents' home for Sunday dinner. (I knew it would be alright for Ma always made enough to feed a tribe!). However, she planned to see her family for dinner, but she promised to stop in on her return home. My ailing grandmother lived with us and was as tickled to see her as I was. Granny was always disturbed that I had not married and here I was 34 years old. Truth be told, I had never seen anyone else I was interested in. I got her address and phone number.

My parents went to town every Friday and were gone most of the day. From that time on, every Friday I raced to get all my chores done so I could visit her before she went to work in the afternoon. I kept quiet about these trysts as I did not want my parents to know quite yet. She came to church every other week because she worked at the hospital the opposite weekends.

The arrival of spring meant I had to farm all through the week; no longer could I break away to visit her. So, she started coming to the farm to help me on her days off. I don't know that we ever had what you would call a real date. We were just content to be together. She seemed to love to work hard, just as I did. When chores were done in the evening, Ma would have a good supper for all of us. After supper, Dad would tip his chair back on two legs and spin 'yarns' (otherwise known as tall tales) from his childhood. Then he would get out his violin and play the old hymns he loved while she accompanied him on the piano. Just good family time. Dad and Grandma saw the handwriting on the wall. I was in love.

Sundays were the best days. We only did the chores necessary to care for the animals, so I had free time. After church, we shared a picnic lunch; she was a good cook, a real plus 'cause I loved to eat. Then we would sit on the grass under that big old maple tree and share our journeys, our cares, and our goals. She wept through her recent struggle with a church split that had truly shattered her emotionally and spiritually. She was still trying to find her spiritual bearings. I couldn't fix it, but I could listen, which seemed to help her.

She related her call to be a nurse and what she supposed to be a call to be a missionary. Even before she graduated nursing school, the doors to missionary service seemed to close. Nevertheless, her passion to see souls come to Jesus did not diminish despite her recent confusion and disillusionment with her church. In our own country multitudes needed to hear about Jesus. Couldn't she be a home missionary? Sadly, health issues plagued her and perhaps were the reason the doors were closing to foreign missionary service. Some unknown malady kept knocking her down physically. It always involved a high fever and a long recuperation.

If God did not plan for her to be on a foreign soil, could it be that maybe He would let her be my wife?

She came for the Christmas Eve service then to our home for supper, 'yarns' music, and games. I didn't want her to leave. Mom and Dad finally went to bed at 11 p.m. At last, I was free to conduct my final order of business. I had to know how she felt about many things that we had not discussed all these past months. However, they were important to me and if there was going to be an issue, I wanted to know about it now.

"What do you think of blue silos?" I asked.

"Oh, blue is my favorite color!" This city girl had no idea that a blue silo meant you spent three times as much money to hopefully have better quality feed for the cows. With further explanation she assured me I would be free to make business decisions.

"What do you think of buying land?' Farming was in my blood. This was most important to me.

"I think it is a good idea." She replied.

My interrogation lasted till almost 2 a.m. We were both getting tired. This time she asked me.

"Do you have another question to ask?"

"Would you like to get married?"

"I thought you would never ask!" And indeed, she had reason to think that.

We got married a month later. Just a simple ceremony with only family present, but we were married. We set the cornerstone of our marriage to honor God in all things. Sunday would follow the tradition of three generations of my family. We would keep Sunday special, not to be legalistic with a lot of rules, but rather with principles. A day to rest and worship; set apart from other days. We planned the day to be special, 'Sunday special.'

"If you turn away your foot from the Sabbath, from doing your pleasure on My holy day and call the Sabbath a delight, the holy day of the Lord, honorable; and shall honor Him, not doing your own ways nor finding your own pleasure nor speaking your own words, then shalt thou delight thyself in the Lord" (Isaiah 58:13-14). It is amazing how this principle kept our lives anchored in Christ. There was so much that could have distracted us and thereby hindered our journey together.

God supplied a great many opportunities for us not only to plant corn, wheat, and beans, but also spiritual seeds, especially into the lives of young people. Some worked for us on the farm. Some were foster children. Others came for farm, school, and church activities. Some were relatives whom we took into our home in time of need. We adopted two special needs children. Many of those seeds produced spiritual fruit.

Our lives were truly blessed. We had almost 41 years together before God called me home. For the last birthday I was with her, I gave her this card:

You are my storybook love,
The woman of my dreams.
And our life together
Is my happily ever after.

"Whoso findeth a wife, findeth a good thing" (Proverbs 18:22).

Chapter 7
THE WATCH

"Watch therefore: for ye know not what hour your Lord doth come" (Matthew 24:42).

"Do you think you could just sit and drive the tractor to till the ground?" My husband pleaded. " A storm is moving in this afternoon and I need to get the alfalfa planted before it rains. I still have to finish the barn chores and feed the animals. Could you just try?" he implored. " I will work as fast as I can and come back to relieve you."

A new alfalfa crop would feed our dairy herd for five to eight years. However, I had been in the hospital critically ill less than one month prior. Doctors only gave me a fifty-fifty chance of survival from the mysterious malady they could neither name nor did they know how to treat. During my illness, my husband struggled to keep up with chores and spring planting while caring for his ailing mother and our recently adopted special needs son. All my heart wanted to help him; however, I was unsure if my physical condition could bear it.

"I will work as fast as possible so I can come back to relieve you. Could you just try?" He was desperate. I didn't hesitate to try but I still had not been able to sit up for even one hour. What I didn't think to ask was how many chores he still had left to do.

Perched on the seat of our red 1086 International Harvester tractor, I braced myself for the first leg of an impossible journey. *Nothing about this would be difficult if I were well,* I told myself. The flat topography of the land afforded me a view of the barn he was working in one mile south of the field. The engine roared in a monotonous drone as it tugged the tillage tool over the hard clay ground. My head bobbed to the hypnotic rhythm. Around and around, I traveled; first north to south, then south to north. Ten minutes each direction. Back and forth, back and forth; as the ground slowly yielded to the pounding of the machine.

As I traveled north, I prayed for strength to make it just one more round. As I traveled south, I scanned the horizon for any sign of his coming. I looked at my watch. The first hour had passed. My energy level depleted just as I had expected. I had no strength left but neither did I have any alternative.

We didn't have cell phones in those days. My only alternative was to stop the tractor and lie on the ground. I struggled to sit erect on the seat. Every time I turned the tractor, the same choice confronted me. Continue or lie on the ground. Collapse on the ground and fail him in his hour of need? I couldn't do it. He promised he would return as soon as possible. He always kept his word. This task had to be completed today. No reservoir of strength had I. My prayer became focused on strength moment by moment.

Leaning on the steering wheel, unable to sit erect any longer I asked myself, *How alike is my situation as watching for Jesus to return?* North to south watching, south to north praying. Watching. Praying. Love bound me to keep trying. With my head now leaning against the steering wheel, I could barely see where I was going. My watch declared two hours passed.

There it was. The fence that marked the boundary of the field. One more time south and the field would be ready to plant. I prayed for strength to remain on the seat; not slump to the floor. Then I saw the billowing dust from his truck tires as he raced back to relieve me. My work was finished. I could go home now.

I achieved what seemed an impossible goal. My grateful husband lifted me from the tractor, put me in the truck and raced back to the house as fast as he had come. He carried me into the house, gently tucked me in bed, then raced back to the field with the planter. He had just finished planting the last round when the rain came. We had alfalfa from that field for seven years.

When I am weary of trials and sorrows, as I walk the Christian way, I
am O' so oft reminded of that trying and difficult day. And lo' as I feel
my strength a -fleeting I can hear my sweet Lord say: Hold tightly to
My promise, child For I am on my way. My loving arms will lift you,
when you can do no more. So many treasures in heaven, for you I have
in store. Your part in the harvest is finished Your work on earth is done.
My precious, lovely daughter To take you home now, I have come.

by Stephanie Judd

"Watch ye therefore, for ye know not when the master of the house cometh..." (Mark 13:35)

Chapter 8
THE SURRENDER

"And this is the confidence that we have in Him, that if we ask anything according to His will, He heareth us" (I John 5:14).

"There is a farm for sale!" my husband announced, his face gleaming with excitement. "It is just around the corner and borders on the home place!" My husband, the diligent, hard-working farmer, frugal and wise, could not pass up a chance to buy more land. His brown eyes danced with delight when he walked out of the realtor's office, mortgage papers in hand. It was my job to worry. He just knew God would provide and he didn't hesitate to tell me so. However, I balanced the checkbook every month and I paid the bills.

I knew the farm economy was in a depression and that we were barely making it without buying more land, but he figured it was manageable. We could pay the mortgage by making an annual payment from the wheat harvest. He scheduled the payments to occur every August. Besides, he reasoned, having more land would increase the total farm income. Yet, I knew more land meant more expenses. I knew crop prices had remained barely above the cost of production for several years.

My husband, the optimist. Me, the realist.

Our discussion took place the previous fall. Now, it was near harvest time. We walked the fields, testing the moisture content as the wheat heads bowed in preparation to surrender their precious content. We anticipated a bountiful yield, but it was not quite ripe.

Boom! The house rattled, startling me awake. It was 2 a.m. Hail pelted the windows. The wheat! A twinge of despair pierced my thoughts. Hail had taken out many a wheat crop before this year. If it took out this crop, there goes the farm! I prayed. As the first rays of sunlight glistened over the horizon, my fears were confirmed. The wheat lay flattened to the ground.

With heavy hearts, we milked the cows, fed the animals and cleaned the barn, all the while dreading the next step. We had to survey the damage. "Look! The wheat is still in the sheave. It wasn't ripe enough to be beaten to the ground! I can harvest it!" my husband exclaimed delightedly. We thanked God for His faithfulness to meet our needs.

The weather forecast changed Sunday afternoon. Monday, another storm, worse than the last one, appeared to be moving in our direction. The wheat truly was ripe and ready for harvest. All our neighbors diligently combined their wheat. Howbeit, we were beset with a dilemma. For three generations our family farm faithfully kept the Lord's Day special. We honored God with worship and rest rather than engage in unnecessary farm work. That 'Sunday Special' vow was the cornerstone of our marriage.

Would financial stress push us, just this once, to break our 'Sunday Special' vow? While our neighbors harvested their wheat, we prayed and sought guidance, or rather, perhaps we sought God's permission to break our vow. God did not give in to our weakness, but rather urged us to trust Him. My husband was at peace. Me-financial heaviness weighed my heart down. We had no other resources to pay that $6000 mortgage.

Monday, 4 a.m. found us in the barn and by 7 a.m. we were in the fields. My husband assessed the challenging situation. "I will have to go very slow. If I am to skim this wheat from the ground, I can only combine in one direction. Pull the truck alongside me when you see the bin on the combine almost full, so I can continue to combine while I empty the bin." I acknowledged my understanding of the instructions and hurried to the adjacent field to bale hay. We needed the hay just as badly to feed the cows the next winter. I balanced the pressure to bale the heavy windrows of hay against the risk of going too fast and causing the baler to break down. A breakdown certainly would not save any time.

All morning, I kept watch of that bin as I baled hay. At the appointed time, I drove my tractor and baler to the corner of the field, ran to the truck, and pulled alongside the combine. We drove in tandem at one mile an hour while he augured the wheat from the combine to the truck. When he needed fuel, I carried a gas can, climbed the back of the moving combine, and refueled for him. Teamwork. We never stopped. Slowly, harvested wheat filled the truck.

I raced back to my tractor and continued to bale. I hoped the storm would hold off till evening. As I felt the dampness approaching, ominous, dark, swirling clouds pierced my hope. I intensified the vigor of my prayers. My fervent prayers sought to convince God just how desperate the situation was. Nevertheless, the Spirit kept whispering back, "Whose wheat is it, anyway?" I groaned, "Yours God, but we need it so badly! We can't make the mortgage payment without it."

The sky loomed darker. Winds howled as they picked up force, twisting my windrows of hay every which way. It was impossible to get it all. My heart was overcome with concern for we absolutely had to have that wheat money to pay the mortgage. There was no other way. We had no spare money. I pleaded and begged with all my strength for Divine intervention. As always, the Spirit answered back, "Whose wheat is it, anyway?" I tried to reason with God, "Well, it's yours Lord. But you know how badly I need it to pay that bill. I have no other way." It seemed God and I just were not on the same page!

At noontime, darkness settled in as thick as a moonless midnight. I turned the tractor lights on. I could hardly see my hand in front of my face, let alone the combine. Gale force winds hammered my face and body as the brunt of the storm moved closer. I realized I was fighting a losing battle with God. It was over! Who can argue with God and win?

Despondent, I surrendered. "It's your wheat Lord, do with it as you will. If we lose the farm, we lose the farm." I had barely uttered those words when, suddenly, the storm clouds split in two. The billowing blackness retreated as one part of the storm rolled two miles south and the other part roared two miles north. A few miles down the road the storm again merged into one black mass and rushed into the next county, leaving tens of thousands of dollars of destruction in its wake. Our farm and the little farms around us were left completely unscathed,

Out came the sun. The day was bright again. My eyes couldn't believe what I had just witnessed! A clear sky opened above my head! The storm clouds rolled away! At the point of surrender, God supplied the needed miracle. God taught me a lesson of obedience and trust. Most important: surrender to His will in all things. Prayer is not rubbing the genie in the bottle to get our own way. True prayer surrenders circumstances to His sovereignty for His glory.

> "But my God shall supply all your need according to his riches in glory by Christ Jesus" (Philippians 4:19).

Chapter 9
The Atheist

"I have no pleasure in the death of the wicked but that the wicked turn from his way and live" (Ezekiel 33:11).

"Why won't you help me? I suffer with unbearable pain, and you won't help me! If I weren't so d—— weak I would go out to the barn and shoot myself!" Steve spit out his disgust. I sat quietly, avoiding eye contact until he regained both his breath and his composure.

It was just a year ago his wife died unexpectedly. They both had been my home care patients. At the time, she was gravely ill. However, he was in hospice for cancer. I recalled many whispered conversations with his wife to encourage her in the Lord as Steve forbade any reference to God in his home.

Amazingly, his cancer remained stagnant and asymptomatic. Therefore, the doctor discharged him from hospice. However, I could not discharge him from my prayers. Unfortunately, now the cancer had returned with a vengeance and was aggressively sucking the life out of him. I was again his hospice nurse.

"Steve," I quietly spoke to get his attention. "I have been trying to get you pain relief, but everything the doctor orders you refuse to take. If you at least tried the medications, we would know if they helped or not. Will you take a pain pill now?" I asked.

"No, I don't want any of your stupid pills!" He edged himself forward a bit in the recliner as his three adult daughters huddled in a corner of the kitchen, intimidated by his aggressive, contemptuous behavior. Anger only slightly strengthened his ability to move. Everything in him cried to be free of this terminal diagnosis. To his chagrin, his anger just would not, could not change his current situation.

"If you won't do anything about this pain, just give me the pill to end it all!" he shouted, his face turning a purplish red. Desperation filled his voice as he pleaded for the only way out visible to him.

"I cannot fulfill your request. First, because it is illegal and second, it is not God's way." The word was out. I said the name 'God' in his presence. Glazed eyes glared at me. I maintained calm eye contact.

"If I could get to Oregon, it would be legal, so there!" He shouted back at me.

Silence.

I began to speak, "You're not the only person who has ever felt this way. Life and death are a bigger story than what you are suffering now. There was a man in the Bible who suffered much. His name was Job. He lived thousands of years ago. He did not understand his suffering either and longed for relief. He faithfully worshiped God and lived his life to please God. What he did not see was the spiritual battle between God and Satan. Satan believed Job only served God because of all the blessings God bestowed on him. God knew the faithfulness of Job's heart. God allowed Satan to steal Job's wealth, slay his 10 children and inflict Job's body with a painful disease. Job, though confused and without knowledge of the battle behind the scenes, kept his trust in God. Through his pain, he confidently declared, "He knows the way that I take, and when he hath tried me, I shall come forth as gold." I paused to let the truth sink in. He kept his head down.

"The battle between good and evil began in the Garden of Eden. I'm sure you have heard the story of Adam and Eve. Only one thing God warned them not to do. Satan, desiring to usurp the Creator God from His throne, disguised himself and placed a question in Eve's mind. Was not God truly withholding something desirable from them? She looked at the forbidden fruit, saw that it was pleasant to the eyes, good for food, and desirable to make one wise. She ate it and then shared it with her husband, Adam. Their eyes were opened and indeed they knew good and evil. God told them if they ate of the fruit of that tree, they would surely die. Sin infected the whole human race with a fallen, or sinful, nature. The wages of sin is death. Suffering and death began then." Steve kept his head down. I continued.

"God's love did not forsake them. He knew this would happen. Redemption's plan was in place before they sinned. God demonstrated His love for them alongside the high cost of sin. He took a lamb that Adam and Eve had cared for and killed it to make clothing to cover their newly discovered nakedness. The lamb shed it's blood and died first, a picture of the death of Jesus, the sinless Lamb of God, who would shed His blood to ransom us from the penalty of sin. The Bible tells us that "without the shedding of Blood there is no remission of sin" (Hebrews 9:22).

"The blood of that lamb could not save all humanity. God's Son, Jesus, the perfect lamb of God, came to earth born of a virgin: fully God and fully man. He demonstrated to the world He was the promised Messiah with many miracles. He healed the sick, cast out demons and raised the dead. John the Baptist proclaimed Him, "Behold the Lamb of God who taketh away the sin of the world" (John 1:29). Only one without sin could take our sin upon Him. Jesus shed His innocent blood to redeem us from eternal damnation. "For God so loved the world that He gave His only begotten Son that whosoever believeth in Him should not perish but have everlasting life" (John3:16). I scanned the room. Perhaps a Bible might be hidden somewhere. No, no Bible. So, I continued.

"When the appointed time came for Him to lay down His earthly life for us who are lost in sin, Jesus didn't get to just take a pill or even a gun. As the religious zealots in holy fervor were on their way to arrest him, He prayed to His heavenly Father, "If it be possible, let this cup pass from Me. Nevertheless, not as I will, but as thou wilt" (Matthew 26:39). Steve appeared unaffected, looking into his lap. At least he was listening.

"Hatred and cruelty found a climax in death by crucifixion. Because people called Him king, they wove a branch of a thorn bush into a crown and pushed it into His scalp. Blood ran down His face and neck. They accused the One who looked on them in love of being a blasphemer. They blindfolded Him, spit on His face and mocked Him. They whipped Him, stripping the skin off his back and chest. That not being enough, they laid the weight of the heavy wooden cross onto his shredded back to carry it to the place of crucifixion. They nailed His hands and feet to that rugged cross. Soldiers raised the cross and dropped into the appointed hole with a thud, jarring all those wounds. He hung there, the weight of the sin of the world bearing harder on Him than all the pain caused by His physical wounds. He could have called ten thousand angels to take Him off that cross and end His suffering. But He chose obedience to His Father, God, to redeem mankind from sin that we might still have a choice to love and serve Him. Remember, without the shedding of blood there is no remission of sin. "For the wages of sin is death, but the gift of God is eternal life through Jesus Christ our Lord" (Romans 6 :23). God's presence was palpable in the room as conviction settled on Steve.

The Atheist broke down in uncontrolled sobbing and repented of a life foolishly spent, love spurned, and relationships lost. His daughters, who prayed for him for many long years, wept with him and praised God for His faithfulness, love, and unending mercy. Heaven came down and glory filled our souls as the angels rejoiced in heaven. A lost soul redeemed.

The atheist, now the Redeemed one, never got out of his recliner. He did, however, leave all pain, suffering and tears behind as he crossed the river to join his wife around God's throne the next morning

> "For by grace are ye saved through faith and that not of yourselves it is the gift of God" (Ephesians 2:8).

Chapter 10
REACH FOR JESUS

"The Lord is nigh unto them that are of a broken heart and saveth such as be of a contrite spirit" (Psalm 34:18).

Weeping uncontrollably, Wanda reached for some –any- hope that she might cling to. She desperately needed encouragement. In just one day, one proclamation, one momentous decision, that 'hope' had dissolved into an elusive dream. She sat on her couch stunned. The consequences of the decision she and her family made just yesterday knocked at the door. It was the hospice nurse.

"I am your hospice nurse," I introduced myself. Through her sobs Wanda returned a whispered acknowledgement. I took the seat offered to me in her homey living room.

"The goals of hospice are to keep you comfortable and give you as much quality of life as possible," I explained. "Please tell me about your journey to this point." I waited patiently for her response.

"Six months ago, I finally went to the emergency room. The chronic cough wore me out and the pain was getting worse. I think I knew it was cancer, so I tried to ignore it. Her words were interrupted to catch a breath. Across the room, in comfortable easy chairs, sat her husband of 40 years and three adult daughters.

A heavy silence settled before she continued. "I tried every treatment offered me even though it made me so sick... I lost my hair. I don't want to die. I'm not ready to die." The sudden burst of energy induced

PORTRAITS OF GRACE

a prolonged coughing spell. Her husband moved closer to her and laid a comforting arm around her shoulders.

"This wouldn't be happening if you would have quit smoking when I was a kid! But no, you just had to have those d—- cigarettes! You didn't love me enough to quit, did you?" the youngest daughter, Maggie, proclaimed.

"You don't understand, Maggie. I needed them. I only reached for a cigarette when I needed to calm down. I didn't want to hurt you. I loved you then and I love you now. I don't want to die! Please forgive me!" Her uncontrollable sobbing seemed no match for the anger of her daughter.

"This is a difficult time for each of you. Each of you has a different perspective and grief to work through. For today, we need to focus on making the most of what time there is left." Maggie got up and went into the kitchen as I continued the difficult discussion.

"No, you won't call 911. Call hospice first with any issues. If we cannot keep you comfortable the doctor will decide if you need to go to the hospital. Are you ready to sign the 'Do Not Resuscitate' form?" Tears welled up in Wanda's eyes.

"But what if I have a heart attack, couldn't I have just a little more time?" she begged with her dusky body shaking from the cough. "Do Not Resuscitate seems so final! So hopeless!"

"The cancer has invaded most of your lung tissue. I can't offer you that hope," I replied. Solemn quiet filled the room.

Two days later I made a follow up visit. Wanda, her husband and two oldest daughters were present.

"Why, oh why, did I smoke?" lamented Wanda. "The girls used to beg me to quit, even when they were in grade school... I was so stubborn. I wanted to do what I wanted to do, and no one was going to stop me. I never took my health seriously; I never took God seriously! And now I am dying!" She sobbed with her head between her knees.

I wrapped my arm around Wanda's heaving shoulders. "Jesus loved you when you did not take Him seriously. Jesus loves you today. Jesus has made a way for you to be forgiven of your sins and spend eternity with

Reach for Jesus

Him." I picked up a dusty Bible from the coffee table. The whole family listened as I laid out God's lifeline of hope. I encouraged them to reach out to Jesus.

As the days went by, Wanda mixed self-loathing with repentance, unable to forgive herself.

"Just reach out to Jesus, Wanda," I reassured her. "He is right here ready to forgive." I opened Wanda's Bible to Romans 5:8. "But commended His love toward us, in that while we were yet sinners, Christ died for us."

"I want God and His forgiveness, but how can He forgive me after I put Him on a back burner all my life?" Wanda objected.

Again, I reviewed the scriptures. "Jesus paid the penalty for your sins because He longs to be reconciled with you no matter what. He loves you unconditionally, more than anyone ever loved you. Just reach out to Jesus. He loves you." Again, I reviewed the Scriptures with her. The Spirit did His work in their hearts. Wanda, her husband and two daughters wept their way to the throne of God's grace. Unfortunately, Maggie was not present.

When I arrived for a visit one day, Wanda sobbed profusely, "Maggie will not forgive me! She is so angry *gasp* and always blaming me. *cough* I wish I could go back in time, but I can't. *gasp* She has been more dependent on me *gasp* than the others. *cough* I think she is *gasp* really scared. *cough* What can I do?" Wanda wept and coughed from the bed that now confined her.

"We can pray. She is not out of the reach of Jesus and the hope He has to offer." I encouraged Wanda and together we prayed.

A few days later, I arrived at their home providentially early. Maggie sulked in the farthest corner of the bedroom while the rest of the family sat by Wanda's bedside. Her shallow breathing was barely perceptible. No one spoke.

Suddenly, her eyes opened but she did not make eye contact with anyone in the room. She did not share any meaningful last words. Rather, she reached one thin arm to heaven. Her husband knelt by her bed holding the other hand. Then, as if she saw Jesus, she lifted her head off her pillow and reached for the unseen Hand. Peacefully, she crossed the river and entered the Promised Land.

"Let not your heart be troubled: ye believe in God believe also in me. In my Father's house are many mansions. If it were not so, I would have told you. I go to prepare a place for you. And if I go and prepare a place for you, I will come again, and receive you unto myself; that where I am, there ye may be also" (John 14:1-3). I quoted the promise.

At that moment, Maggie broke down and sobbed. The anger left her as she ran to her father's open and forgiving arms.

> "He healeth the broken in heart and bindeth up their wounds" (Psalm 147:3).

Chapter 11
THE WORDLESS WITNESS

"I have planted, Apollos watered; but God gave the increase" (I Corinthians 3:6).

"There she is," Cheryl muttered, peering out her gray sheer curtains as she took one more puff before opening the door. One more puff. Didn't matter anyway. The damage was done. The doctor told her to quit smoking. He had told her that for years.

"Hi, Cheryl," I greeted, trying not to choke on the smoke in the room. "Your doctor sent me to help you take care of those leg ulcers." Cheryl directed me to a chair in front of her recliner. Pink fluid dripped from the dressings her doctor placed just yesterday. Underneath the bandages, ruddy, swollen skin appeared ready to rupture. She turned her head nonchalantly and lit another cigarette. "I need these cigarettes to calm me," she stated as smoke engulfed me.

Cheryl kept up her incessant chatter, broken only by puffs on the cigarettes she kept lighting. I quietly worked and listened. It seemed Cheryl did not need any answers, only someone to listen. Ceramics were her thing and she had quite a collection of statues and pots sprinkled around her humble but neat trailer. As I was leaving, I took time to admire her handiwork. I wanted to build a bridge of connection.

I smell like a smoldering fire, I mused to myself as I walked to my car. *Even the fresh air doesn't help.* I was thankful this was the last visit of the day. I would not want to go anywhere else smelling like a smoke bomb. I prayed, "Lord, help this dear lady. Love on her through me."

Every day I prayed for Cheryl. Every day I made nursing visits. Every day Cheryl kept up her incessant chatter. Every day smoke encompassed me as I worked. Every day I drove away feeling spiritually defeated. "Why can't I find even one little opportunity to tell this lady about you, Jesus?" I cried.

Amazingly, the wounds that the doctors said would not heal, did heal despite Cheryl's continued smoking. On my last visit to discharge her from home nursing care, Cheryl surprised me with a gift. A beautiful blue ceramic angel she made for me. How precious! As I left her home for the last time, I broke down in tears. For a full year I had been a failure. Not once had I found a way to tell Cheryl of the love of Jesus! *Why? Why? Had I missed a cue from the Holy Spirit?* I felt guilty and defeated. What I didn't know was that this story of God's grace was not finished.

One evening, ten years later, my husband and I went to a Saturday night hymn sing at a small community church. During intermission, a short, middle-aged lady approached me and inquired, "Do you remember me?" The voice sounded familiar, but no, I could not place her.

Cheryl proceeded to remind me of our history: the horrible wounds that took a year to heal, chain-smoking and the ceramic angel. I was shocked beyond belief! Cheryl's radiant smile lit up the room.

"What happened?" I quizzed. "You don't look like the same person!"

"I am not the same person!" Cheryl exclaimed! "I got saved six months ago. Since that time, I have been delivered from cigarettes," she continued, "You planted the seed when you were my nurse. Later, God sent someone else to water it. Then God gave the increase, and now I am a child of the King!" A triumphant smile confirmed her witness. Blessing and rejoicing broke out as we embraced, sisters in Christ! God had spoken without the use of my lips! He had answered my prayers.

Six months after this glad reunion, Cheryl's obituary appeared in the newspaper. Although her earthly life of fifty-five years appeared to have been cut short by her addiction, Cheryl's eternal life with her Savior had just begun.

"Be still and know that I am God" (Psalm 46:1).

Chapter 12
Precious in His Sight

"Precious in the sight of the Lord is the death of His saints" (Psalm 116:15).

"I am not going to stay here! They should have just kept her at the hospital!"

"Neither am I! It smells like poop! I'm gonna puke!"

Thud! It sounded like someone hit their fist against the wall.

My knock at the door interrupted the chaos inside, albeit, it did not cease. "I am the nurse here to care for Joyce," I shouted to be heard above the clamor.

A young man escorted me into the living room. There lie, or rather tossed about, was Joyce. Garbled, incoherent speech ran non-stop. Joyce's non-verbal communication revealed her intent to get her approximately hundred-pound body over the bed-rails. I rushed to hinder her efforts. However, calm speech did nothing to conciliate her behavior as she did not follow directions.

She was just forty-nine years old when surgery to remove her stomach cancer turned out worse than anyone expected. Following the surgery, her family received the hard truth. Joyce had two weeks or less to live. Comfort care was the most they could expect after her entire stomach was removed. She would never eat again.

Joyce was the anchor for her family. Without her stability, raw emotions lacked boundaries. Chaos and combativeness reigned.

No wonder they are so overwhelmed. I thought as I surveyed the vast amount of medical paraphernalia scattered in boxes around the room. One IV line supplied nutrition. Another IV delivered Morphine to control the pain. Drains from her abdomen filled thick dressings with foul smelling gunk. Adult diapers seemed insulting. They were clueless about the other medications to control her agitation. Besides, who would be at her bedside, the bed she was continually trying to escape from?

It took me two hours just to manage her IVs, medications and dressings. This situation needed order for her family to be competent to care for her. A nurse would come in every twelve hours to manage the IV and medications and to make dressing changes. Nevertheless, they needed to learn a lot quickly.

Having finished my nursing tasks, I scanned the angry and troubled faces of her husband and adult children. They granted me respectful silence as they gathered around the kitchen table. I shared with them the precarious state Joyce was in and emphasized the need for a peaceful, quiet environment. After providing written instruction and ascertaining their understanding, I broached what I felt was a core issue.

"Considering the state she is in, there may be a spiritual issue troubling her. May I speak to her about her spiritual condition?" In unison, they gratefully agreed to any intervention that may help her.

"Lord, how can I tell this lady of your love in the mental state she is in?" I prayed as I traveled between patients the next day. It would take a miracle.

Joyce's husband greeted me at the door that evening and escorted me to her peaceful room. Unexpectedly, Joyce greeted me warmly and in her right mind! Suddenly I realized I did not pray in faith for I was totally unprepared for the change of events.

"What do I do now, Lord?" I prayed. I performed my nursing tasks for the next two hours while the Holy Spirit guided our conversation. Joyce listened intently. That night, she asked Jesus to forgive her sins. In childlike faith she became a child of the king.

Joyce was discharged from the hospital with a life expectancy of two weeks or less. Those two weeks passed, and she was still alert. One day the Holy Spirit whispered to me, "She is never going to be able to go to church. You need to disciple her." From then on, every night I shared Bible stories with her while I cared for her, tasks which always took two hours. She listened with rapt attention and asked questions. Each night before I left, we prayed together.

Soon thereafter, Joyce's mother also became a Christian and began to read the Bible to her daily. However, as her spirit grew in the Lord, Joyce's body declined.

"My daughter is engaged to a wonderful man." she told me one evening. "I know I will never see my grandchild, but I would like to make something for him. I could give it to my daughter for Christmas." I wanted to help her make her last Christmas special.

With the help of my teenage daughter who drove the car and the wheelchair, I managed all the medical paraphernalia to take her to a dime store. For just a short hour, it was almost like she wasn't sick. She bought small gifts for every family member. But what could she do for the not-yet-conceived grandchild she would never see? What special gift could she get? She decided to make a handcrafted gift of love . She chose a yellow blanket with blocks she could embroider. Incredibly pleased, but exhausted, her last excursion to the outside world was complete. Christmas climaxed her end-of-life deeds for her family.

In January, Joyce's decline accelerated. She slept most of the time. Incredibly, when she was awake, she was alert. One evening in mid-January, I arrived to find her holding her Bible. The Bible that her blurred vision always prevented her from reading.

"Would you like me to read to you?" I asked, reaching for the open Bible. I started to read where my eyes first landed. "Precious in the sight of the Lord is the death of His saints."

We both knew it was her time. We rejoiced for a few minutes in His wonderful salvation. Afterward, Joyce slept because she could not stay awake. I finished my tasks in tearful quietness. While I was happy for her, we were as close as sisters and surely I would grieve her absence.

As I left the home, I shared with her husband that this may be the night she would go to be with Jesus. Tearfully, he took the mattress from his bedroom and laid it on the floor beside her hospital bed. Gently, he lifted her sleeping form from the hospital bed to the mattress. He laid down with her and held her in his arms till she moved to the arms of Jesus at 4 a.m. Precious in the sight of the Lord is the death of his saints.

> "And God shall wipe away all tears from their eyes: and there shall be no more death, neither sorrow, nor crying, neither shall there be any more pain; for the former things are passed away" (Revelation 21:4).

Chapter 13
The Divine Detour

"A man's heart deviseth his way; but the Lord directeth his steps" (Proverbs 16:13).

"You're fired!" declared my boss unapologetically. I could not understand how my action could be considered a HIPPA violation; moreover my fifteen years of dedicated service could not hold a candle to the serious error I had made. Now, I was fired one month before I was scheduled to take the certification exam for Hospice and Palliative care.

The Divine Detour *embarks.*

"Now what do I do?" I sobbed my way to the throne of grace. For over a year, I had studied for the exam. On top of that, I had already paid the $400 non-refundable fee.

"Cast thy burden upon the Lord and He shall sustain thee. He will never suffer the righteous to be moved" (Psalm 55:22). 'Stay the course' seemed the answer God gave me.

A friend of mine worked at a nursing home where they needed staff, so I took an "as needed" position to help. One day, a nurse aide who worked there told me of an opening at a hospice house about an hour away. I applied with my hospice certification in hand. Two months later, the call finally came.

"You're hired if you still want the position," stated the caller. "We need a Certified Hospice nurse." I accepted the position.

"I have a dream," I remember sharing with the manager with whom I worked most closely.

"And what might that be?" he asked. I hesitated to answer for it truly was a big dream.

"I would like to open a non-profit hospice home... a place where services would be free. The poor and those with no one to care for them would be cared for with dignity and comfort at the end of their life. I saw such a need for it in my rural community when I was doing home hospice there."

He thought for a minute before responding. "There are two such places within an hour of here. I will speak to them about working with you on this project." Fortunately, the management team I was employed with was excited to equip me for this daunting task. My employer gave me increased responsibility and opportunity, as well as connected me with resources and experienced business-people.

The Divine Detour educates.

Two years had passed since that 'you're fired' day. I was still in the role of as-needed staffing at the nursing home while employed with the hospital-based hospice house. Government mandates on how to care for nursing home residents who were near the end of life lacked understanding and compassion.

One resident, blind and deaf, tall and weak, was obviously a candidate for hospice, yet he was not on a hospice program. Perhaps, he had two months to live. Out of compassion for his weakened condition, I instructed the aides to put him in a Geri-chair (a reclining wheelchair) for breakfast. When the Director of Nursing came in and saw him in the Geri-chair, she scolded me and informed me that it was against the law. She put anti-tip legs on a regular wheelchair for him.

The next week I arrived for a morning shift at the nursing home. We had just started the morning report. Thud! I looked for the source of the noise. There he lie, face down in a pool of blood. The blind and deaf man, tall and weak, lie in his own blood. The wheels of his wheelchair spun, suspended above his prone body. The anti-tip mechanism did not compensate for the center of gravity of his tall body. I raced down the hall. Leaning over his twisted body, I screamed on the inside, but cried on the outside. "God, if you don't want me to start a hospice house, you must stop me! I cannot take seeing this type of thing anymore!"

The Divine Detour *engages.*

Instead of stopping me, God told me the steps to take, one at a time, during my morning prayer time. First, I placed an advertisement in a local newspaper to invite anyone interested in starting a hospice house to attend a meeting. Twenty people showed up. These dedicated people became the core steering committee for the Hospice House.

Within fifteen months, by prayer and God's guidance, we cleared all governmental hurdles, obtained a non-profit status, and completed the creation of our policies, procedures, and documentation forms. A local businessman volunteered to underwrite a property when we found one with an affordable land contract.

The Divine Detour *enables.*

Everything appeared ready to go. We put a bid on what we thought was the ideal property. God protected us from a bad decision when the seller backed out a few hours before we were to close.

"But our ways are not God's ways" (Isaiah 55:9).

Now I prayed, "Lord, direct our path. What house do you want us to have?"

> "In all thy ways acknowledge Him and He shall direct your path" (Proverbs 3:6).

On my way home one day, I noticed a 'For Sale' sign in a yard that I hadn't noticed on my way into town. People were in the yard, so I pulled in and inquired. It had only been on the market for one hour!

This was the house that God had chosen. It combined a peaceful country setting with a homey interior. It was close enough to town to provide natural gas for heat, yet far enough into the country to have a well and septic system thereby eliminating a water bill. Guests and families could appreciate the wildlife in the backyard and the peacefulness of the country setting. God does all things well!

The Divine Detour *established*.

> "I will instruct thee and teach thee in the way which thou shalt go;
>
> I will guide thee with mine eye" (Psalm 32:8).

Chapter 14
NOT ABOUT HYPOCRISY

"What shall it profit a man, if he shall gain the whole world, and lose his own soul? Or what shall a man give in exchange for his soul?" (Mark 8:36-37).

"David, I'm afraid we found something we were not expecting." The doctor matter-of-factly stated. He avoided eye contact with his patient as he prepared to report the findings of the open and close abdominal surgery.

"You have stage four colon cancer that has metastases throughout your entire abdomen. There is nothing we can do. You have only two to three months to live. You best get your affairs in order." The surgeon rushed out of the hospital room to avoid any further contact, leaving David stunned.

I'm only fifty-six years old and never been sick a day in my life till now, David thought to himself. *How could this happen? I will face this like a man?* he told himself. He presented his plan to the doctor. "If I go to a hospice house now while I am still able to care for myself, I can get to know the people and I think it would be easier for me when the end does come." His doctor agreed and arranged for his admission to the hospital-based hospice house David had chosen. Thankfully, finances were no obstacle as he was a prominent businessman and politician.

David's congeniality and contagious laughter caught the nurses and staff off guard. He was so alive! He enjoyed joking and familiarizing

PORTRAITS OF GRACE

himself with his new surroundings. His magnetic personality accomplished his goal. This wasn't so bad after all.

The first two months passed uneventfully. Laughter resonated through the halls, as his fun-loving friends who came to comfort him left smiling. Perhaps it was not true. Maybe the doctor was wrong. How could he have so much fun if he were dying?

Month three started a steady demise with less energy and much less laughter. The dark, gray cloud of cancer encroached on his luminous personality. Creeping grief invaded the hearts of the nurses who now had to address his increasing need for comfort, understanding, education and support.

Sunday morning dawned bright and pleasant, but the atmosphere had changed. David's call light was on. He had never used his call light. I had arrived early for my shift and took advantage of the opportunity to help him. He was too weak to make it to the bathroom. His demeanor was also changed, but it was shift change and I did not have time to make a meaningful interaction.

All day long I kept watch of David's room for an opportunity to address this transition with him. He was not my assigned patient for the day, so I had no casual interchanges with him. Besides, those in my charge needed my attention. All day long his daughter sat with him. All day long she never left his room. Just before shift change that evening, his daughter left. I seized this final opportunity.

"This morning, when I helped you to the bathroom, I couldn't help but notice something different about you." I broached the topic of change.

"Your right, nurse, there is." He responded. "I am getting weak so fast, and I don't have an appetite. I feel a bit nauseated all the time and that seems to be getting worse. Will I have to suffer a lot while I am dying?" he asked, struggling to maintain his composure. "And the pain is getting worse also."

I responded reassuringly, "David, it is important that you tell us what you are feeling. We have medications to keep you comfortable.

I am confident we can control your pain and nausea, but only if you tell us." Then I pressed on to another area where my heart felt he really needed to talk. "But I feel like there is something else, something more, perhaps something spiritual, that is bothering you."

"Your right, nurse, there is," he replied again. "You see, as a boy I was raised in church. I was taught the right path, but when I left home, I turned my back on it. Now as I know I am dying; it just seems so hypocritical to ask God for forgiveness when I chose to use my whole useful life without Him." Tears threatened to tumble down his cheeks as he struggled to control his emotions.

The Holy Spirit prompted me, "It's not about hypocrisy, David. It's about reconciliation. Your daughter spent the entire day with you. Now, consider, if either of you had had a falling out and had not spoken for several years, and then one of you received a terminal diagnosis, would you not want to be reconciled before you lost the opportunity?" His facade of strength left him, and he began to openly weep.

"That is exactly what has happened to me! My daughter and I had an argument two years ago and she had not spoken to me since. Today she spent the entire day with me," David recollected.

"God wants the same thing for you. He wants you to be reconciled to Himself. He loves you, David." At that point, I was called away. His heart had been watered.

I was off for the next few days. Upon my return to work, everyone greeted me with the same message from the politician who had passed away. "He asked me to tell you he found Jesus."

A few days later, the night nurse who was on duty when David found Jesus, filled in the blanks for the rest of the story. Around shift change, a group of Christian men came to visit him. To them, God gave the privilege to reap the harvest.

David had repented of his sin and found the grace of God to be all sufficient. What rejoicing there had been in that hospice room that night; for another wandering soul had been safely secured in the fold.

PORTRAITS OF GRACE

What singing and rejoicing had rung through the halls! Hallelujah what a Savior! Imagine the rejoicing in Heaven. A sinner has come home!

> "If we confess our sins, He is faithful and just to forgive us our sins and to cleanse us from all unrighteousness" (I John 1:9).

Chapter 15
THE ANOINTING

"In whom we have redemption through His blood, the forgiveness of sins, according to the riches of His grace" (Ephesians 1:7).

"No! No! No! A wail came from the hospital room at the end of the hall. The lone occupant had quite abruptly been confronted with her own mortality.

What could have happened? She had awakened that morning quite prepared to move to a rehabilitation facility. Now, a death sentence had been pronounced on her. She cried and cried and cried, totally unable to grasp the change in her situation.

I responded to the first referral to the Hospice House by going to the hospital to meet our potential first guest and to introduce her to the Hospice House. Her medical team of physicians, nurses, a social worker, and an intern were all gathered in the hall just outside her door. I approached and introduced myself. Some of the team had tears in their eyes as they related the symptoms of her recent decline.

"She is appropriate for hospice and for the Hospice House," I agreed. "Has anyone told her she is dying?" They all hung their heads. "She is such a nice lady; we just can't tell her," blurted out one of the nurses.

"But someone must go in and tell her she is dying before I meet her. I cannot go in and tell her about Hospice House if she does not even know she is dying!" I pressed them until one member of the team reluctantly agreed. Then came the wailing.

I waited a few minutes. She was still sobbing when I quietly entered the room. I gently took her hand in mine, and waited for her to acknowledge me.

"I am a nurse from the Hospice House," I said as I introduced myself. "Arrangements have been made for you to come to our facility this afternoon. I have come to tell you about the place and answer any questions you might have." I waited.

"If I go to that hospice house; I will only live a few days!" Though she did not realize it at the time, her feelings of anger were mingled with truth.

I stayed with her that first night at Hospice House. She slept quietly. Not knowing what to do, I sat in a recliner near her bed in the shadow of a night-light. I listened for the rhythm of her shallow breathing as I prayed. At about 1 a.m. she awoke.

"It's so nice to have someone to talk to when I wake up in the middle of the night!" she exclaimed. And talk she did. She talked of her family, her children, and her current situation. She continued her life review until she butted up against a dark place. A place that had changed her life, her outlook, and her destiny. A place that had presented a spiritual challenge to her for all her adult years. Confession was easier with a stranger in a dark room in the middle of the night. This was the 'great sin' she thought she could never be forgiven of.

"Oh, dear one, Jesus loves you so much. He never wanted you to run from Him. He shed His blood on the cross to pay the price for your sin. Come to Him! The Bible tells us Jesus came and took our punishment in Ephesians 1:7, "In whom we have redemption through His blood the forgiveness of sins according to the riches of His grace."

I hesitated while she sobbed and then continued. "First John 1:9 promises, 'If we confess out sins, He is faithful and just to forgive us our sins and to cleanse us from all unrighteousness.' He assures us in John 3:16, 'For God so loved the world, He gave His only begotten Son, that whosoever believeth in Him should not perish, but have everlasting life.'

He loves you! He is waiting to forgive you. He wants to take you to heaven to be with Him."

Tears flowed freely. "I did not think He could ever forgive me! I cannot forgive me! Such an awful thing!" Heavy sobs interrupted her. "I was raised in the church. I have no peace and I am dying!" She wept uncontrollably. For more than fifty years this burden of sin had weighed her down. It robbed her of the peace and joy Jesus would have given. It robbed her of a life she could have lived for Jesus.

"Would you like me to pray with you?" I offered.

"Yes." We prayed. The weight and grief of her sin disintegrated as she wept a Kleenex box full of repentant tears. Jesus came and washed her sins away and made her whiter than snow. With the burden of sin erased, her spirit soared to the heavens rejoicing. His Holy presence descended on the Hospice House. Mercy, grace and love filled our hearts.

> "For Godly sorrow worketh repentance to salvation not to be repented of" (II Corinthians 7:10).

She settled back into a peaceful slumber. Sun rays seeped into the room in the early morning hours, and she awakened with the deep-seated joy of the Son radiating from her soul.

Sharing Jesus marked the last mile of her earthly journey. Friends and family joined her in joyful praise, singing hymns and worshiping the Lord of Lord and King of Kings until her strength waned and a deep settled peace abode over her unresponsive body.

God had set His anointing on the vision and mission of Hospice House.

> "For God, who commanded the light to shine out of darkness, hath shined in our hearts, to give the light of the knowledge of the glory of God in the face of Jesus Christ" (II Corinthians 4:6).

Chapter 16
THE BIG QUESTION

> "These things have I written unto you that believe on the name of the Son of God, that ye may know that ye have eternal life, and that ye may believe on the name of the Son of God" (I John 5:13).

"I have an urgent need for a placement," the hospice agency nurse related by phone. "He is a ninety-year-old man with end stage cancer and has no family to care for him. His nurse found him too weak to get out of bed this morning. Do you have a room?" We did have room, allowing Jim to arrive by ambulance a few hours later.

"Hi Mr. Brown," I greeted him as the stretcher transported him to his room at Hospice House. The ambulance crew shifted his weak body from the stretcher to the hospital bed as he took inventory of his new surroundings. Sheer white curtains framed the windows of the warm turquoise room with peaceful country scenes displayed on the walls. Blue Jays and Cardinals jostled for position at the bird feeder just outside his window. *This is where my life will end,* he thought to himself.

"Let me help you get comfortable, then I will give you some time to rest, Mr. Brown."

"You can call me Jim, everyone does," he responded.

"Then Jim it is. We do not have scheduled mealtimes here. You can have something to eat whenever you want it. Are you hungry now?" I queried.

"I haven't had much of an appetite lately. I will try a little, but don't bring much. Sometimes, if there is a lot of food, I get nauseated just looking at it." His voice trailed off into silence.

Such a quiet man. He never complained or asked for anything. I tried to break the silence with a little chatter or soft music in the background. For as long as he had a little strength to sit up, I transported him in a wheelchair to the recliner in the living room, especially for breakfast. He loved watching the wildlife scamper around the idyllic backyard setting.

"It is Sunday morning, Jim. Kinda pretty out for January. At least the sun is shining," I chatted as I got him settled in the recliner and served him his favorite, steaming hot Cream of Wheat. True to his quiet nature, he looked about, feeling no pressure to respond to what I just said.

"Sunday morning. Yep. The wife and me, we used to go to church every Sunday morning for sixty-eight years." He sat pensive.

A sacred quietness filled the moment. "It was just a little country church. The one I grew up in," he continued. "We never had any kids. Wished we could have." He paused again, deep in thought. "I didn't have any siblings, my wife only had one sister. That sister only had one son, my nephew. He is the only relative I have, and he lives quite a distance away. Since she went to be with the Lord five years ago, I have been so alone."

A sense of emptiness hung over the room as he took small bites of his hot cereal. His pain of grief needed the healing balm of heaven. Healing balm doesn't need words. Jesus, the Man of Sorrows, is the Lord of grief. He understands our loss and pain.

He resumed; his voice more hushed, "I have wanted to go and be with her since that day. I wondered how my end would come. Now this cancer..." He sat for a while watching the birds and rabbits. Instrumental hymns played softly in the background.

That was the last time Jim was strong enough to get out of bed. He wasn't hungry and He only needed a few drops of liquid for his dry mouth and the pain medicine to keep him comfortable. He rarely spoke other than to mutter a 'thank you.'

As I re-positioned him in bed a week later, he asked, "Will I make it?"

"Make it where, Jim?" I asked.

"To heaven."

"Do you love Jesus with all your heart, soul, mind and spirit?" I asked.

"Yes, I do," he replied firmly, without hesitation.

"Has Jesus forgiven you of all your sins?" Again, he answered affirmatively without hesitation.

"Yes, you will make it, Jim," I replied just as adamantly. "The Bible tells us 'that if thou shalt confess with thy mouth the Lord Jesus and shalt believe in thine heart that God hath raised Him from the dead, thou shalt be saved' (Romans 10:9).

Another place Jesus tells us, "In my Father's house are many mansions: if it were not so, I would have told you. And if I go and prepare a place for you, I will come again, and receive you unto myself that where I am, there ye may be also" (John 14:2-3).

After our conversation, Jim closed his eyes and never spoke again. He left his cancer-ridden body to return to the dust of the earth with a smile on its wrinkled face, for his spirit now rejoiced with his Father in the heavenly realms.

> "Now the God of hope fill you with all joy and peace in believing, that ye may abound in hope, through the power of the Holy Ghost" (Romans 15:13).

Molasses Cookies oven 375 F

Bake for 12-14 min.
Mix ¾ cup lard or margarine, softened
¾ cup sugar
Add 1 egg and beat into sugar/lard mixture
Add ¾ cup molasses
Sift 3 ½ cup flour
1 tsp. Salt
1 tsp baking powder
2 tsp. Cinnamon
1 tsp. Ginger
1 tsp. baking soda

Alternately add the sifted flour mixture with ¾ cup sour milk.
Mix only until blended. Do not over mix.
Drop by tablespoonful on a greased baking sheet.
Flatten with a cup that has been dipped in sugar.
Makes approximately 36 cookies

Chapter 18
THE FINAL GIFT

"The Lord God is a sun and shield: the Lord will give grace and glory: no good thing will He withhold from them that walk uprightly" (Psalm 84:11).

"I never expected to be here so soon," Doris lamented. "I thought I had a little more time." Her mildly retarded son, David, sat silently in the corner of the room.

"Nurse, I need to settle some legal things before I die so David is cared for. My lawyer is on vacation this week. I made an appointment for next Monday not dreaming my condition would decline so rapidly. Do you think I will make it?" she asked meekly.

"You may still be alive, but the big issue is, will you be alert? You are in a lot of pain…It might be a wise choice to get another lawyer," I suggested.

"He already has all the information. All I need to do is sign the papers. Please help me make it! David needs the house and support. I don't think I have the information for another lawyer anyway."

"We will do the best we can," I told her, thinking-*this will take a miracle.*

Our conversation took place on a Monday. The lawyer would not arrive until the following Monday at noon. I knew Doris' cancer required a lot of pain medication. I prayed, though I did not believe she could be alert that far into the future.

David touched my heart with his quiet simplicity. "Lord, I know from experience it is not likely she will be able to sign those papers next week.

We need your intervention if this is to happen." This request became my daily prayer.

Thursday found her barely communicating. David sat by her bed barely responding himself. It was hard on him. Her dying wish needed to be fulfilled, although it seemed an impossibility.

"Lord, what can I do?" I called the hospice agency and received new medication titration orders which would slowly decrease the dose of a sedating drug while increasing the dose of a similar, but less sedating drug. I doubted it could help but I had to try something. David's future hung in the balance.

Friday morning: Doris gave no response to stimuli.

Friday afternoon: She voluntarily held David's hand.

Encouraged, I continued the titration.

Saturday morning: She opened her eyes.

Saturday evening: Garbled speech. Pain controlled.

My faith aroused. God directed our path.

Sunday morning: Awake, speech clear. A bit confused. Pain controlled.

Sunday evening: Awake and alert. Stated she had some pain, but it was bearable.

"I think I can make it and sign those papers!" Doris happily exclaimed upon learning she had only eighteen hours to go. We continued to pray. Now, we had more faith. Staff kept the current dosage schedule through the night as her dying wish weighed on us.

It was Monday morning. "I will hold your 8 a.m. medications so you will be able to sign the papers. We will not move or disturb you in any way that would cause increased pain. As soon as the paperwork is finished, we will give you what you need to be comfortable."

"Oh, nurse, thank you so much! Thank God that I can do this!"

Doris spent those precious hours with David. Bittersweet it was for him, cherished moments with his mom, a special part of her final gift.

At the appointed time, her attorney arrived. Thirty minutes later she was ready for comfort care to resume. Her 'house now in order', her heart was at peace. Her last good-byes said.

The Final Gift

That evening, no response. David stayed by her bedside. Early morning, angels came for her.

> "All things whatsoever you shall ask in prayer, believing, you shall receive" (Matthew 21:22).

Chapter 19
THE PAINTING

"I Am the way, the truth and the life, no man cometh unto the Father but by Me" (John 14:6).

Caught in the vice-grip of addiction, Sandy had lost everything. This vicious cycle of loss fueled an even greater dependency on illegal drugs and alcohol. Now, at just forty-one years of age, her body had had enough. It could no longer rebound from the relentless abuse. She was dying.

She came to Hospice House from the hospital. Comatose, with multi-organ failure, doctors could no longer summon a positive response to any treatment. She had no power of attorney to speak for her, no family to sit with her to share fond memories, and no friend to be faithful to her. Alone, she was dying.

Not much medical history came with her. Addiction had held a jealous love for her. Many drug pushers had relieved her of her finances, her independence and her dignity. Addiction demanded she love their destructive effects more than family, friends, and even her only son.

Two other residents were at Hospice House at the same time as she. Although they had vastly different backgrounds, they had lived their lives for Jesus and had produced fruit in their lives of service for the Kingdom. Their children honored them and praised God for His blessings. In their final days, family and friends often gathered in the living room. Around the piano, they harmonized hymns of mercy and deliverance, grace and truth, and the hope of Heaven. The Holy Spirit inhabited their praise and bound the hearts of these two families together on hallowed ground.

One evening, a knock came at the door. Standing at the entrance was a thin young man who appeared to be in his early twenties. "Do you have someone named Sandy here?" He inquired.

"Yes, she is here," I replied. The young man informed me that she was his mom whom he had not seen since he was taken into foster care at the age of seven. He had never been adopted and had aged out of foster care when he turned eighteen.

"Could I see her and maybe even sit with her for a while?" he asked.

I led him to her room while giving him an explanation of her condition. I encouraged him to talk to her as hearing was the last of the senses to leave the body. All the visitors in the house overheard his sad story. A spirit of prayer settled on them, and the music stopped as a hallowed silence settled in. Sandy's son sat with her for an hour or so and left after asking if he could come back.

He returned the next day to sit with her again. As the other families gathered around the piano, one of them invited him to join them. He welcomed the comfort and camaraderie. They loved him and he felt like he had a family.

On her last day, Sandy's son sat with her all day. She was actively dying. No one knew the effect the Spirit of God had on her, for she never responded. However, as she was drawing her last breath, a smile appeared on her face, a moment of joy mixed with sadness for that abandoned son! The other families shared his grief and his joy.

None of us realized just how deeply the atmosphere had affected him until a few weeks later when he returned to Hospice House with a picture for us. A picture he had painted and framed in memory of his mom and their time at Hospice House. Looking at the picture made one feel they were walking down a beautiful path through a woodland. The bright sun was setting at the end of the road. Butterflies flirted amongst the tree branches. Sandy's son explained that this was how he felt when his mom was dying; she was walking down the path to eternity. That picture still hangs on the living room wall at Hospice House as a vivid reminder of the grace, mercy and love that brought peace to a troubled journey.

> "I am the light of the world; he that followeth me shall not walk in darkness but shall have the light of life" (John 8:12).

Chapter 20
ONE SPECIAL NIGHT

"I go to prepare a place for you" (John 14:2b).

"Why does she just keep lying here, dying but not dying?" Marian asked, fatigued from the week-long watch of her mom lingering in a near death state. "She hasn't known us or even spoken a word for seven years! Can she even think?"

"Dementia has been such a long hard journey for all of us," another daughter, Cheryl, commented. "If she had not gotten this cancer who knows how long she might have lived."

"She is ninety-three years old, only skin and bones now, and hasn't even had a drop of water in over a week. How long can this go on?" Bonnie, the youngest of the three daughters ventured to ask what they all wanted to know.

"I do not know how long she will linger." That was the only answer I could truthfully give. "I have witnessed people with dementia linger for thirty days or more with absolutely no food or fluids even when they have been nothing but skin and bones like your mom."

"Could we get a minister or someone to come and pray with her and with us tonight? Perhaps she needs some kind of peace and comfort," Cheryl posed, "At least it may help us, and we will be doing something rather than just helplessly sitting here."

It took a few phone calls to find a minister able to come on short notice. He arrived about 9 p.m. We all gathered around her bed as he began to read scripture from John 14. "I go to prepare a place for you. If it were not so I would have told you." His soothing quiet voice brought peace to their anxious hearts. Jesus offered the hope of heaven. The minister offered a prayer for comfort and ended it with the Lord's prayer. Amazingly, their mother prayed the Lord's prayer in unison with him. She had not forgotten the words. When the last amen was said, the demented lady who had not spoken in seven years proclaimed, "That was awesome!" Three daughters shot shocked glances at one other. Seven years she had not said a word and now she not only speaks but remembers the Lord's prayer!

We escorted the minister, who was equally shocked, to the door and thanked him for coming so late and on such short notice. I returned with her three daughters to their mother's room where she was still talking, but not to us. More than that, she was seeing, only not us. She began to proclaim in amazement the wonders only her eyes could behold. Her radiated joy and excitement were contagious.

"Oh, it's so good to see you!" She exclaimed, reaching a hand heavenward and shaking it in greeting.

"Look at that!" She pointed toward the ceiling.

"Awesome!" Now her attention was directed to a corner of the room. We stood spellbound on holy ground as we watched her tour the place that would soon be her home.

"How beautiful! Isn't that amazing!" Four hours passed. We dared hardly to breathe as she previewed the marvels of eternity. Her excitement faded as her energy declined. Soon she took her first breath of heavenly air. Heaven is real.

Hospice House: Heaven's birthing room.

> "For thou art worthy, O Lord, to receive glory and honor and power; for thou hast created all things, and for thy pleasure they are and were created" (Revelation 4:11).

Chapter 21
Hope Redefined

"Thou wilt shew me the path of life: in thy presence is fullness of joy: at thy right hand are pleasures for evermore" (Psalm 16:11).

Day 1:

Today, I arrived at the Hospice House.

Real sheets on the bed! Birds feeding outside my window! This is perfect! I had no idea what to expect when I left the university hospital to come to Hospice House.

I had not even heard of this place though I have lived within a few miles of it for the last decade. There was no one to care for me at home so this was a practical choice. This room is so like my bedroom at home, I can hardly believe it! I knew God was guiding this journey even though this is not the journey I had been praying for.

Day 2:

I need to connect with my children and make sure their hearts are right with God. I miss my wife. It's been twelve years since she passed away from cancer. She was so young. I wish I had been a better support to my children. I guess I thought they were young adults and could manage their grief. My personal grief overwhelmed me so badly that I failed to be a good support for my children. I guess kids are always closer to their mother. No matter how it happened, there are several rifts in the family. We are just not close anymore.

Day 3:

Six months ago, when the doctor told me I had skin cancer, he said they would be able to get it all. I was not sixty years old yet. I saw no reason to worry about it. God is so good that He would see me through this trial. Now, I seem to be dying and I can't grasp this reality.

Day 4:

How time changes perspective. I always hoped in God. I have loved and served Him for almost forty years now. I believed and hoped to serve Him for many more years. I hoped to see my grandchildren grow up. I hoped to travel. I hoped to have many more hunting and fishing trips. I hoped. I hoped. I hoped.

When the cancer progressed, I hoped for healing. I believed God would heal me and I would give Him all the glory. Faithful saints in my church joined me in believing prayer, just like we are instructed in James 5:14-15. We claimed this promise: "Is any among you sick, let him call for the elders of the church: and let them pray over him, anointing him with oil in the name of the Lord: and the prayer of faith shall save the sick and the Lord shall raise him up."

I just do not understand. All the treatments that they said would heal me have failed. I am in Hospice House. I can't understand how this could happen. I had faith. I believed I would be healed, but now the pain is excruciating.

I think I can identify with the torments of Job and say as he did 'my days are spent without hope.'

Hope Redefined

Day 5;

I am thankful to be in a Christian place and that I can sense God's presence here. Most of the staff love Jesus as I do. I talked with one of the nurses last night and told her I didn't want to die. I'm not ready to give up hope. I know God could heal me any day He chooses. However, she gave me a different perspective. Was my prayer of faith in God's will or in my own will? Perhaps my suffering and imminent death were according to the will of God.

She read to me I Peter 4:19, "Wherefore let them that suffer according to the will of God commit the keeping of their souls to him in well doing, as unto a faithful Creator."

As I prayed this morning, God gave me a redefined hope. I hope to demonstrate trust in God in this hard place, especially for those who have no faith or those whose faith is weak.

My first step of redefined hope will be reconciliation with my children who have distanced themselves from me. I need to know about their spiritual welfare. I need to assure them of my love and acceptance of them.

I will call each one of them today. I guess it is not a lack of faith to admit I am dying. They need to know. I don't need to punish them by having my death be a shock with no chance to make things right. I know God will give me grace and wisdom for these conversations. He promised.

My redefined hope will demonstrate to my friends and fellow Christians God's faithfulness even when we don't understand. By God's grace, there will be no more chaffing under this trial nor anymore questioning of God. I need to encourage those who come to visit me, not have 'pity parties.'

My redefined hope will give God glory for all the wonderful things He has done for me and my family. I want Him to be glorified through this illness. He abides with me.

I am so close to heaven, but my failures and selfish behaviors loom so heavy on me. God forgives me but it is hard to forgive myself. I wish

I had lived closer to Him all my days. I wish I had spent more time in prayer. I wish I had become more like Him.

Day 6:

I will call my hunting and fishing buddies if God will give me enough strength. I must tell them I had my last trip with them. I want them to remember how good Jesus is. I want them to know that to surrender to His plan brings perfect peace. I have said and done things I now regret. I wish I had shown a more Christ-like attitude. I wish I had always had the peace of God that I have now.

Day 7:

This will be my last entry into this journal. I need relief from this excruciating pain. I will start taking the pain medication they offer me. At first, I didn't want to. I wanted my mind to be clear to 'put my house in order'.

I thank God for how He has helped me. My son from out west is coming. I don't think I will live to see him. We both cried when I talked to him on the phone. Such regrets that we left unfinished business go for such a long time. We both let our egos rob us of the relationship we longed for.

There will be no more good times with him on this earth. It's too late now. I must let this grief go. I pray that God will be glorified in the legacy I leave my children. When they clean out my house, they will find the Bibles I marked in for each one of them.

Note from the nurse:

Your pastor came when your pain was unbearable. He prayed with you as the medication began numbing your senses. He told you this was as bad as it was going to get, and he was right. Your son got here an hour before Jesus took you home. You left a smile on your disease-scarred face as you took the hand of Jesus. That was a comfort to him.

Your redefined hope gave a faithful witness to your family and friends and to all at Hospice House, that we can trust God even when we don't understand. You showed us your redefined hope through reconciliation with your family, even as we are reconciled to God in Christ Jesus. Your redefined hope gave glory to God as you surrendered to His sovereignty. Your eternal life of pain-free joy in the Lord is just beginning. Your legacy lives on. Thank you for sharing. I will never forget you.

> "For this God is our God for ever and ever; He will be our guide even unto death" (Psalm 48:14).

Chapter 22
The Challenge

"For the weapons of our warfare are not carnal, but mighty through God to the pulling down of strongholds" (II Corinthians 10:4).

"Get out of here, all of you! I hate you! I hate you! "Thud!" Resounded from behind the closed door. Donna had been at Hospice House for two weeks. Congeniality usually beamed from her engaging smile and sparkling eyes, but this time her trembling daughter, struggled to sweep up the shattered pieces of wet glass and yellow flowers. Not only was the vase shattered, but also her daughter, Wendy's inner being. What was happening? As quickly as the barrage had started, it abated, and her mom returned to her cheerful self.

Not realizing what occurred, I wedged myself into the 'crowded to overflowing' entrance of Hospice House on my day off. All three beds were occupied. I came to companion a dear friend and benefactor of the Hospice House on the last leg of his earthly journey. At ninety years of age, this quiet man with a passion for missions was soon to receive his crown to lay at his Savior's feet.

Before I got to his room, I met Wendy, maneuvering a slightly tilted dustpan, apologetically between on-comers. Not noticing the contents of the dustpan, I wondered, *why is she trying to clean right now with so many people here?* As quickly as the thought came, I let it go. I had reached my destination.

My dear friend's wife of forty years held his hand as she struggled to hide her tears and verbalize her final gift to him by releasing him to their Savior. He was taking his last breath on earth as I entered the room. Immense grief, wrapped in Heaven's joy, cradled the peaceful transition. A sacred silence memorialized a life well-lived. We sat where words have no meaning, and the Comforter enfolded our numb and aching hearts with an unexplainable peace.

Suddenly, Donna erupted again! I quickly took my exit to find the reason for the awful screaming. She sat upright in her hospital bed; her glaring eyes penetrated me. Frustrated that everything she might weaponize had been removed from her reach, she banged on the bed rails and welded her fists as viable options to execute her wrath. She screamed obscenities laced with damnation to everyone in the room.

I hastened to bring medications to calm her, but she vigorously refused. Trying to remain calm to quiet the clamor, I explained we only wanted to make her feel better. I gave her time to process what I said, but she did not need time. She screamed at the top of her lungs, "You're all trying to kill me! You're trying to kill me!"

"This exact same thing happened just before you got here," Wendy sobbed. "Without provocation or explanation, she became violently angry with all of us daughters, grasped a large vase of flowers and pitched it across the room at us. It shattered into a million pieces..." *So that was why she was cleaning the room at such an inconvenient time.*

Like a thundercloud racing to eclipse the sun, Donna's bright eyes became dark and sinister. Her voice changed from its gentle feminine nature to a husky deep, even venomous tone. The voice directed itself at me as evil permeated the atmosphere.

"What are you CHRISTIAN WOMEN trying to do here, anyway?" the accuser challenged.

"Donna, it is the Blood of Jesus that saves you from sin! The Blood of Jesus! The Blood of Jesus!" I directed my words to the victim of the sinister voice. "The Blood of Jesus! The Blood of Jesus! "In Whom we have redemption through His blood" (Colossians 1:14). "It is the Blood of Jesus that saves us! The Blood of Jesus saves!"

When the evil one could stand it no more, he departed as suddenly as he had appeared.

Donna again spoke in her normal tone of voice, seemingly oblivious to what had just happened. Her daughters and friends trembled from the effects of the terrifying encounter.

In one room, the Comforter had come. Down the hall, the accuser had come. In the end, Jesus came as Lord of all. The end of life is the last battlefield of the soul.

> "For we wrestle not against flesh and blood, but against principalities, against powers, against the rulers of the darkness of this world, against spiritual wickedness in high places" (Ephesians 6:12).

Chapter 23
THE BLOOD

> "Wherefore He is able also to save them to the uttermost that come unto God by Him, seeing He ever liveth to make intercession for them" (Hebrews 7:25).

"Do you have any beds available?" the caller asked with a sense of urgency in her voice.

"Yes, we have one bed," I responded. "What is going on?"

"Our nurse just arrived at a client's home and found her lying on the front porch, bleeding," the hospice agency social worker responded. "Her husband threw her out of the house, quite literally, and locked the door. We are going to file an elder abuse report against him, but we need a safe place for her to go right now."

An hour later Judy arrived by ambulance. I watched as the ambulance crew transported her by wheelchair up the entrance ramp. Her head hung low, due whether by weakness or shame, I did not know. She came with nothing but the ragged, dirty, bloodstained clothes on her back. No personal items. No medications. No self-respect. Her frail, cachectic body was covered in blood, both fresh and dried, from her face to her feet.

I left her in her room still in the wheelchair to get pans of warm soapy water. *How could anyone do this to someone they had pledged to love, especially when they were sick unto death?* I started gently soaking the dried blood to prevent even more tearing of her paper-thin skin. Gradually, the blood washed away only to reveal the old bruises and injuries in various stages of healing. .

"I have been sick for so long; it has been hard on my husband," Judy began. "This last month I just could barely walk, and I could not even prepare him a simple meal. To tell the truth, nothing sounded good, so I couldn't even think of something to prepare. I'm not hungry anymore." I listened. My heart was angry. *How could anyone be so abusive to another, let alone to someone who was dying!*

"For some reason, I think he was just frustrated with my long illness, he got really upset this morning. He really is a wonderful man. Please don't think bad of him for this. It's just been too hard for him," she pleaded.

"This has been very hard for you, too!" I responded. "I am so thankful you are here. We want to help you and keep you comfortable. People can be so cruel when things get hard, or when they are threatened in some way." She made no response. "We are all born with a sinful nature. Sin is what pushed your husband to act so badly. The curse of sin has hung on mankind from the moment Adam and Eve disobeyed the one thing God told them not to do. At that moment their innocence left them and a sinful nature entered their hearts. Just like a child, when they understand right from wrong, they tried to hide their wrong-doing. When God came to walk with them in the garden during the cool of the evening, He knew what they had done." She listened, staring at the floor.

"God's love could not abandon His dearly beloved, but disobedient children. He killed a lamb to make clothes out of the hide. The death of that innocent lamb gave them a picture of the cost of sin. The Bible tells us that 'without the shedding of blood, there is no forgiveness of sin.' That lamb was a symbol of the Lamb of God, Jesus, who at the appointed time would come to earth to pay the debt of sin we owe. Jesus suffered at the hands of the sinful people He came to save." Again, I paused, while her gaze remained steadfast on the wet floor, wet with the remnants of blood and water that dripped from my cloths.

"God told Adam and Eve that disobedience would result in death. The Bible tells us the wages of sin is death and eternal separation from God.

We all sin and deserve eternal separation from God. The good news is God promised us a gift if we would receive it. The gift of God is eternal life through Jesus Christ."

"Jesus Christ, the Lamb of God, came to earth as a baby; the babe in the manger that we celebrate at Christmas. When He became an adult, He served others by relieving pain and suffering, healing the sick, raising the dead, giving sight to the blind, and casting out demons as well as many other signs and wonders. He did all these miracles to prove that He truly was the Son of God. Multitudes followed Him and He taught them about the Kingdom of God." I changed the dirty water while she sat quietly still staring at the floor.

"Sin in the hearts of people makes them cruel and wicked. People were cruel to Jesus also. Hatred and jealousy drove the religious leaders to want Him dead. The multitudes who had followed Him either turned and ran or joined the crazed crowd to cry 'crucify him.' They accused Him of blasphemy because He claimed to be the Son of God. How quickly did they forget all the miracles He did for them. Cruelty, the fruit of sin, had him tortured, shedding His precious blood. True to His purpose in coming to earth, He yielded Himself to be crucified: the Lamb of God, the sinless sacrifice. He paid the debt for our sin that we are unable to pay. The Bible tells us, 'Without the shedding of blood there is no remission of sin' (Hebrews 9:22b). Jesus rose from the dead on the third day, Sin and death were defeated by His death and resurrection. This is what Christians celebrate on Easter. If we believe and trust in Him, He promised to forgive us our sin and take us to be with Him in heaven when we die."

I finished cleaning her up and clothed her in one of our pretty nightgowns. She looked like a different but still very sick lady. I tucked her in bed and left her to rest. She spoke not a word to me the entire day. She would only nod her head 'yes' or 'no' to my questions. The next day she asked me, "What do I have to do to get out of here?"

"You need a competent caregiver and a place to stay." Her eyes fell in disappointment.

Wow! I thought. *I must have come on too strong yesterday!*

No one came to visit her. The hospice agency informed me her husband had been jailed. I did not tell her. The Hospice House staff lovingly cared for her. Still, she kept quiet. The hospice agency nurse came daily. She barely spoke to anyone. She took only sips of fluids and comfort medication. For two days she did not speak to any of the staff. She just lay in bed, sometimes in a fetal position, while her eyes followed the activity around her.

"She started talking last night," Ann, the night nurse, reported when I came in to work one morning. "She said no one ever cared for her like we have. I told her we love Jesus, and we love her. His love flows through us. That is what she sees."

"Judy asked a lot of questions last night about God and forgiveness," Trudy remarked the next morning when I came in. Judy never asked me a question. She was always silent and avoided eye contact with me while I cared for her. I respected her desire for silence. She was talking to the night shift.

One week later, "Judy asked Jesus to forgive her sins and take her home to be in Heaven with Him." Ann had the blessing of leading Judy to the foot of the Cross. We all rejoiced with her. From that time on Judy rapidly declined. The next day she didn't respond to us. Two days later she left her diseased physical body with a smile on her face when Jesus welcomed her home.

"For the redemption of their soul is precious" (Psalm 49:8).

Chapter 24
The Vision

"Thou hast visited me in the night. Thou hast tried me" (Psalm 17:3b).

My heavy knees dropped anchor to the floor beside my unmade bed. Tears that had been bound up by a false front of professionalism burst through my emotional prison.

"So many Lord. So many! I can't do this. I am so empty." I collapsed in a heap, weeping, on the cold hard floor until I had no more strength to cry. *How can I do another twelve-hour day? How can I comfort another grieving heart? How can I watch even one more death?*

"I just can't Lord, I can't! Lord, DO YOU HEAR ME? ...I am so empty... Hear me, please hear me." My raspy voice tapered to a whisper. "Please Lord, hear me." Clutching the mattress, I dragged my frail, 100-pound body onto the bed. Tonight was the eve of yet another Easter that I could not worship in church. How many years had it been? Seemed I was always at Hospice House. The ache in my heart wrapped like a blanket around me as I pulled up the covers and drifted into an exhausted sleep.

Everyone had been excited to start this non-profit hospice house. Several nurses, aides and volunteers had enthusiastically and fervently worked to get to that wondrous grand opening. We had so many people to help back then. Every one of them had worked together for the common mission, but that was six years ago.

Over the years, the reputation of Hospice House had spread throughout the state until we had to turn away many in need for lack of space. Sadly, as the ministry had increased, the base of volunteers had decreased; some had become ill; some had passed away. As volunteers aged, just as I had, they had less energy and dropped off the radar. Efforts to attract more staff had proved futile.

A prisoner of hope, I had trudged on and on and on...

Hope that God would provide a way.

Hope for strength for each day.

Hope to be alert to His leading.

As hope had dwindled so had my will to go on. A hole had been drilled in the 'bottom of my barrel' of hope. Dark clouds of despair eclipsed the Son.

As I drifted into a restless sleep, the recorder of my mind composed scenes of Easters past... "On a hill faraway, stood an old rugged cross..." Tears of gratitude swelled in the eyes of the redeemed as they sang and remembered; it was for our sins He suffered, bled and died.

"Up from the Grave He Arose!" resonated through the sanctuary and bounced off the walls. The redeemed rejoiced to sing "Victory in Jesus." 'Glory to the Lamb of God that taketh away the sin of the world.'" A crescendo of worship rose to bless the heart of God.

The choir sang "He could have called ten thousand angels to destroy the world and set Him free." He could have, but He didn't! Jesus chose not to avoid the bitter cup of torture and humiliation. Rather, because of His everlasting love and unending mercy for fallen man, He remained true to the mission the Father sent Him to accomplish. God so loved the world. Such love!

Crisp, shekinah glory embraces the worshipers. Voices, distant voices, rumble, but from where? Listen. Closer and closer. Louder and louder! Look! The voices are coming from a multitude clothed in white raiment, marching as they sing! Their robes appear white as the light that surrounds them yet distinct. Closer and closer they come, till the voices become quite clear. "Worthy is the Lamb that was slain to receive power, and riches, and wisdom, and strength, and honor and glory, and blessing!" "Worthy is the Lamb! Worthy is the Lamb!"

The Vision

The procession swells as they advance steadily toward the Throne. Thousands by ten thousands line the horizon, until a multitude no man can number, onward marches. "Thou art worthy! Thou art worthy! For Thou hast redeemed us to God by thy blood!"

Mountains tremble as the foundations of the earth shake with the vibrations of the redeemed voices praising the lamb that was slain! Clothed in white raiment, bathed in the glory of Heaven, the throng approaches the Throne and falls prostrate before the Son of God who sits on the throne. Grateful praise and adoration swell, 'Worthy is the Lamb. Worthy is the Lamb." I look higher still. A rainbow crests the Son. The rainbow, the sign of God's promise...

A rooster crows, rudely intruding into my consciousness. *No please! Let me stay with the throng!* My heart instantly pleads. It couldn't be a dream! I was there! I saw it! The rooster crows again. It is morning on earth. Easter morning. The sun sparkles over the eastern sky as the heavenly scene fades. It was only a dream. Or was it a vision?

I bounce out of bed. "I have seen it! I have tasted what awaits me in heaven! Oh, it will be worth it all! Oh, what glory that will be, when my Jesus I shall see!" The words of that old hymn swell in my heart as I hurriedly prepare for another long day.

Today would be different, for I had seen the Lord. Today, I would be a bridge of God's love to the dying in my care. Today, Jesus would be high and lifted up.

Today, my heart is full. Today, my cup overflows. Today, He restores my soul.

The Joy of the Lord is my strength. Mercy, grace and love flow and overflow as worship channels through my hands to care for the dying.

> "Whither shall I go from thy spirit? Or whither shall I flee from thy presence? If I ascend into heaven, thou art there: if I make my bed in hell, behold, thou art there. If I take the wings of the morning, and dwell in the uttermost parts of the sea; even there shall thy hand lead me, and thy right hand shall hold. me" (Psalm 139:7-10).

Chapter 25
One More Bowl of Cornflakes

"For thou, Lord art good and ready to forgive and plenteous in mercy unto all them that call upon thee" (Psalm 86:5).

Cindy sat Indian style in the middle of her hospital bed; her face buried deep in the palms of her hands. A tsunami of emotions flooded her deepest soul. No words, no words, no words! "How could I have done this to myself? How could I have done this to my precious children?"

Cindy's happy childhood had literally gone up in smoke the night of that horrible house fire. Who could have imagined that life would change so quickly? Especially at fifteen years of age. Horror like that only happened in the movies, but this nightmare she had not been able to awaken from. Daddy didn't make it out.

At first, it had been deep sadness mingled with a numb kind of 'going through the motions' of life. Grief counselors met with her at school. At home, she and Mama suffered so deeply, yet so grievously different. They could no longer communicate, let alone comfort one another. The world around her, too soon, returned to 'normal', while grief continued to cut a deeper and deeper chasm into her heart and soul.

Ruthless drug dealers, disguised as friends, identified her as their next profitable victim. "This pill will help you to sleep and get some relief from your pain," they offered. Out of the 'kindness of their heart,' that one little pill was free. Sweet numbness! Sweet rest! Relief provided in just one little pill.

Soon there was a nominal fee for that little pill, but it was worth it. Too young to understand, too alone to seek help and too naive to realize what was happening to her, she sunk deeper and deeper into drugs for comfort and solace. Soon, Heroin became her savior from the deep, dark pain of grief.

"That's what happened to my wife," Rusty concluded the history of his high-school sweethearts' now impending demise. "I tried so many times to protect her from those viscous drug dealers, but I was no match for what that friend, 'Heroin', did for her."

"We married shortly after high school and had three beautiful children. She loved them so much and loved being their mom. Several months at a time she would be drug free. Yet, in the trials of life, drugs were her fallback. She didn't intend to take this path or to damage her body. Most certainly she does not want to be in this situation. She never dreamed she would be an addict, much less face an untimely death because of her addiction."

"Two years ago, the university doctor informed us that the drugs had severely damaged her liver. Her only chance would be a liver transplant," Rusty continued. "I was excited, for there was hope after all."

"Not so fast." the doctor cautioned. "This liver failure is caused by drug abuse so she has to be clean for one year before she can be put on the transplant list."

"Armed with hope, she checked herself into a drug treatment center. Even though she would miss that Christmas with her children, it would give her so many future Christmas holidays. This was her second chance. While she was in treatment, I found a house two hours away and got another job so when she got out, there would be less chance of drugs finding her." He hung his head in silence.

"Then in one weak and foolish moment, her destroyer tempted her. For nine months she had been clean. She might have gotten by with it,

One More Bowl of Cornflakes

but a random drug test caught her. She had to start over again." He hung his head, trying to hide the unbidden tears.

"That was just two months ago. Her liver function has spiraled downward since then. I took her back to the university doctor when her eyes looked yellow to me. He told us she was hospice appropriate."

"I didn't want the children to watch her die. That's why I wanted her at a hospice home. Thank you for taking her in. I will bring the children on weekends." With that, he wrapped his jacket around him and lowered his head against the cool rain and falling leaves.

So that is Cindy's story, I thought to myself. I made time to sit with her daily, listened to stories of her children, and held her while she cried, sharing God's love and forgiveness.

"Could you get a minister to come talk to me?" She asked a few days later.

A local minister came and shared the gospel of forgiveness through the shed blood of Jesus. He prayed with her. Though God forgave her and assured her a home in heaven, she could not forgive herself. The minister came every day to encourage her and to pray with her. Between pastoral visits, she cried almost all her waking hours.

Saturday came. Family day. Into the Hospice House bounded twelve-year-old Sharon, ten-year-old Mandy and six–year-old Andy. So happy to see their mom, laughter rang out as they told all the stories of school from the past week. Rusty stood in a corner and solemnly looked on.

"Can we have something to eat with mommy?" Mandy asked. I gave them all a bowl of cornflakes, including Cindy, because they wanted mommy to eat with them. Cindy struggled to hold her head up and to hide the tears that were pressing for release. No, she would give them this memory. Little Andy did not want it to end.

"Can I have one more bowl of cornflakes with my mommy?" I obliged him to have one more bowl of cornflakes. When they had finished eating, Rusty encouraged their last good-by's and kisses. I followed them outside as he ushered the children into the car. When they were all buckled in, he turned to me and said, "We won't be back. It is too hard."

With heavy grief wrapped around my heart, I returned to find her wilted form sobbing, sitting Indian style in the bed. Quietly, I held her as a mother would hold her grieving child. No words, no words, no words.

> "For the wages of sin is death, but the gift of God is eternal life through Jesus Christ our Lord"(Romans 6:23).

Chapter 26
THE ESCAPE

"Neither is there salvation in any other. For there is none other name under heaven given among men whereby ye must be saved" (Acts 4:12).

"Oh no!" Why are two ambulances here? I only accepted one patient and I only have one bed!" I raced out the door. I had to fix the problem before they tried bringing two patients into Hospice House. *Could I have forgotten I accepted one patient and then accepted another?* I questioned myself, for I knew I was becoming a bit forgetful in recent months.

"Would you please tell me who the patients are that you are bringing? I only remember accepting one lady and I only have one bed."

"No lady, we only brought one patient. This one is a handful. They sent my rig for backup in case they needed help with her."

"What do you mean? The lady has Lou Gering's disease and is partially paralyzed. How could she possibly need four trained EMS to help her?" *What could be going on here?* I puzzled.

"You will see. She is powerful for being partially paralyzed. She terrorized the people at the nursing home. Her fowl mouth has invoked a state investigation against them." With that, four people started to remove the stretcher from the back of the ambulance. Two people handled the stretcher and the other two worked to keep the lady on the stretcher.

Indeed, she had little use of her lower extremities, but she made up for it with enough force and determination in her upper body to undermine anything that was being done for her. Amidst a barrage of cussing, swearing, wild accusations and flailing poorly controlled arms at them, she was finally in the bed with the side rails up. With a final quick gesture of 'good luck', they rushed for the safety of their rigs. What had I gotten not only myself, but all the staff of Hospice House into!

"Lord, guide me. I've never seen anything like this before." With a twinge of despair, I laid the case at the feet of the only One who could handle it. Thankfully, her room was a distance from the other three rooms. I could close the door to muffle her screams, but how could we handle her out of control rage and her craftiness at finding ways to escape? Besides, there were three other patients that needed care.

The nurse from the hospice agency arrived soon and filled in the details behind the transfer. "No one has been able to deal with this lady. She estranged herself from her entire family by her behavior. I think she is so angry with this disease that she somehow thinks by a force of her will, she can escape the gradual debilitation. I have watched her. As the paralysis progresses, her rage increases."

I sat quietly soaking it all in. By all our admission criteria she should not be here. Why didn't they tell me this on the referral? Of course, they knew we would not take her! But the weight in my heart told me she was here by design, through God's providence.

When the hospice nurse left, I went in and just sat, listening to her constant accusations, foul name-calling and swearing. Most of what came out of her mouth was not decent to even repeat.

Thankfully, she can't move her legs. I thought to myself.

So, hopefully, she can't fall out of bed. I prayed. She needed Jesus. Her only escape would be Salvation. That would only come as the Holy Spirit prepared her heart and mind. Every chance I got, I sat quietly by her bed and prayed.

She obviously was in pain, so, I took her some liquid medication to give her some comfort.

"I have some medicine to make you more comfortable." I tried to get a word in between her tongue lashings. She spit it in my face with unbelievable force. Nothing we did seemed to help.

Seven torturous days passed, not only for the staff, but for our 'lady'. Every day the paralysis climbed the nerves and muscles of her body, all the more to torment and imprison her mind. Strength to vent her frustrations faded and her voice softened.

I took the opportunity of her silence to begin to tell her of the love of Jesus. She shot daggers at me from her eyes. I could almost read the labels on the daggers. *If Jesus loves me, why do I have this disease?* and *Is this God's cruel punishment!*

I knew Jesus' presence surrounded us, but the battle raged in the only part of her body not affected by the disease, her mind. I called a local pastor to minister to her.

The pastor sat by her bedside and shared the sufferings of Jesus for her sin. He shared the great love of the Savior for over an hour, most of which I was too busy to overhear. As he was preparing to leave, I heard him say, "Whatever you do, don't die without Jesus."

When I came the next day, she was different. The anger was gone. No more dagger eyes. Her body relaxed. She could no longer move her eyelids to answer a question 'yes' or 'no'. A settled peace wrapped like a blanket around her useless body. She was dying.

When Jesus took her hand to lead her home, I thought a weak smile crossed her face. She had found her escape in Jesus.

"Believe on the Lord Jesus Christ and thou shalt be saved" (Acts 16:31).

Chapter 27
THE LILY

"Consider the lilies how they grow: they toil not, they spin not; and yet I say unto you, that Solomon in all his glory was not arrayed like one of these" (Luke 12:27).

She has been a good wife to me all these sixty years. And, God, you have been so good, especially to me. He thought to himself, as he sat near the window, watching the birds flutter from feeder to feeder.

"Yes, nurse, God has been good to us." He started to tell me their story soon after his wife was admitted to Hospice House.

"You know, I didn't know what to do when the doctor told me she had dementia. I had noticed her becoming more and more forgetful. Still, it shocked me, the diagnosis I mean." He didn't need encouragement to continue. "So, I asked the Lord what I could do to help her. I knew it would be a hard journey, but I never could have imagined how hard."

"We both loved flowers. However, she especially loved lilies. I thought to plant a lily, but plant it in a hard place for it to thrive, because dementia would be a hard place for her to thrive." I nodded.

"I planted it among the hedges under the living room window. The soil there was hard, and the lily struggled to survive. That plant sent its roots deep. Just like we would have to set our roots deep in the Word and trust Jesus to see us through this. I didn't water it either. I determined not to water it. God sent the rain and the lily stretched up through that hard place where I planted it." The memory of that miracle brought a smile to his face.

"As dementia robbed more and more of her memory, that lily kept coming back year after year. You know, nurse, it grew taller than the hedge as it reached toward heaven. She could see the beautiful bloom from the living room window. Such an amazing thing. Her words failed her, but Jesus, the Lily of the Valley, never failed."

She had one to two months to live when she came to Hospice House. This would be the most difficult part of the journey for them both, especially for him. Being nearly ninety years old, her husband lacked the physical strength to care for her at home.

She had been with us a couple of weeks when he asked, "I see there is a lot of spring yard work that needs to be done. Do you have someone that usually does that?"

"No," I responded. "God sends volunteers to help us with it. It is not usually the same group year after year."

"Would it be alright if I got my family, I mean my children and grandchildren, to do that next Saturday?" Of course, permission was gratefully granted.

God provided the perfect weather for that 'family day'. He brought an entourage of young and old, all hard workers. Everyone loved this mother, grandmother, aunt and cousin. I wheeled her out onto the deck in her wheelchair and set up breakfast for her. A daughter sat with her to feed her. Her ambitious family raked and trimmed, cleaned flower beds and anything else they could see to spruce the place up. She watched them working together and laughing together. All was well with her family.

I saw her body start to wilt and we put her back in bed. Something was different, however. Her demeanor changed. She slept.

"I can't get her to wake up," her husband announced when he came in the next morning.

"She has been asleep since I put her back to bed yesterday," I told him. He sat with her, sang to her and read the Bible to her. Still, she slept. Other family members came and talked to her. Still, she slept.

The next day when her husband came in, I told him, "she still has not awakened. Saturday, when she watched you all working together harmoniously, it seemed contentment came over her. Perhaps, she saw you would be alright if she went to be with Jesus. Her work on earth just may be done."

"I knew it was coming... I will miss her." He dabbed the tears from his eyes as he walked, shoulders hunched over, to her room. It was well with her soul. The Lily of the Valley transported her to her heavenly reward.

> "I am the Rose of Sharon and the Lily of the valleys" (Song of Solomon 2:1).

Chapter 28
THE BIBLE AND THE BEAR

"Thy word is a lamp unto my feet and a light unto my path" (Psalm 119:105).

"We have a lady that probably won't last 24 hours. She has suffered a massive stroke and is unresponsive." The hospital discharge planner continued, "Her only relative is a brother who lives some distance away. Do you have a bed?" After I ascertained that she met admission criteria, we scheduled transport for early afternoon.

The ambulance crew wheeled the stretcher into Hospice House. I touched her cold and purple hand. She surely would not be with us long. I pulled the sheet back to aid transfer to the bed. Suddenly I recognized the twisted, emaciated form lying before me. It was Jean. Her dad passed away at Hospice House two years ago. She walked two miles every day to see him, her effort made more pronounced by her twisted, humped-back frame that leaned on a cane for support the whole distance.

Staff and visitors had offered her rides home, which she had always declined. She did take the nourishment we offered her. I remembered a comment she made to me then, "I feel so loved when I come here." Now, two years later, the 'loved one' had returned to the place of His love.

She lived through that first night but remained unresponsive. *It would only be a matter of hours or maybe a day,* I thought. However, our ways are not God's ways, nor do we know His plans.

Seven days later:

"You'll never guess what happened last night!" The night nurse, Andrea, reported to me that morning. "I was coming out of a room, and I heard a noise behind me. It was Jean! She was out of bed, standing in the hallway using the door-frame for support!" She gave me a minute to comprehend what she had just said. I rushed to Jean's room, and was shocked to see her sitting upright in bed and very much alert! It was a miracle! Andrea resumed her report, "I asked her what she was up to and she responded, 'I want to see where I am and what is going on'." *Of course you do!* I thought as I pondered, *How in the world could she come back to life like that?*

Every day Jean gained strength. Her mind was sharp. Every Bible she saw when she walked through the house she took to her room. She loved to read the Bible. Even more she loved someone to read it to her. Between staff and volunteers, we were able to accommodate her desire. Everyone focused on her basic understanding of the simple Bible truths that would lead to salvation. She told us she had not been in church since she was a child.

"How can I know I will go to heaven when I die?" she would ask. Her heart opened to the truth one day. She found the joy of salvation. Fellowship in God's Word marked her days. One month passed. She could walk without a cane and ate well. She was not dying.

"Jean, I have good news and bad news." I tried to gently introduce my subject. *Who knew it would be so hard to tell someone they were not dying!*

"You are doing so well; it appears you are not dying at this time." She beamed. "The bad news is, you are doing so well that you no longer qualify to stay at Hospice House," I continued. "Arrangements are being made for you to transfer to an assisted living nearby."

Her head fell into her hands. Tears soaked her lap. "But I love it here! What will I do without you all? Who will read to me? Who will pray with me?" I held her close to comfort her as a mother comforts her child. She would not be comforted.

It took a few days to make the transfer arrangements. It was during the Covid-19 pandemic era. "Can I take this Bible with me?" She pointed to the Bible that was the most precious to me in the whole house, the white

Bible in the box with the dove on it. The dove, the symbol of peace, was the symbol of Hospice House. I gave it to her.

I needed to do one more thing for this one who had become a sister in Christ; I decided to get her a stuffed animal. In July, stuffed animals are not easy to find. Finally, a thrift shop yielded a bear with a heart on it. Perfect.

The appointed day of departure arrived. With her precious Bible in hand, we wheeled her to her brother's car. I promised to visit her even if I could only visit through the window. Suddenly, it hit me. She would probably have to wear a mask. I grabbed a mask for the bear and presented it to her when she was comfortably seated. "I will hug this bear and pretend it is you." She sobbed.

The assisted living did have strict restrictions which prevented non-family members from visiting. However, Hospice House staff were able to stand outside her window and cheer her on. She always had the Bible and the bear with her.

Six weeks later, her brother called. "I went to see Jean this morning. I walked into her room. She didn't respond to me. She was lying in the bed clutching the bear to her heart, and the Bible lay beside her. She was gone." She left without a word. She had laid up the true Word in her heart.

> "Thy Word have I hid in my heart that I might not sin against thee" (Psalm 119:11).

Chapter 29
THE GRATEFUL HEART

"But thou, O Lord, art a God full of compassion, and gracious, long-suffering and plenteous in mercy and truth" (Psalm 86:15).

"Do you have a bed for a homeless lady who is dying?" The voice on the other end of the line was a hospital discharge planner. In God's providence, we did have one bed. She arrived that afternoon with her husband by her side.

Cheryl sobbed all the way to her room at Hospice House. "I can't believe this is happening to me! My doctor just told me while I was getting my Chemotherapy treatment today that the treatments are not working. They are out of treatment options for me. The treatments made me so sick I thought surely, they were working. Without any time to think about it, he put me in hospice care. He sent us here because we are homeless. I'm only forty-five years old. How could I be dying of this colon cancer?"

"It's all my fault. If I just wouldn't have lost every job that had health insurance. You see nurse," her husband Ralph continued, "we were just dating when she was diagnosed ten years ago. I had a good job back then and I knew that I loved her. We married so she could have health insurance. Everything looked good. The treatments were working, and we thought she would make a full recovery."

I listened with a heavy heart as they did a life review of everything that had gone wrong.

"It's not your fault the shop closed, and I don't blame you for it," his wife interrupted. "You did the best you could. I am so tired now, could I please just rest awhile."

We left the room to allow her to rest. Ralph continued to tell the story of their descent through healthcare loopholes.

"Finally, we moved to Colorado, and I found a really good job with benefits, However, it took three months for the health insurance coverage to go into effect. I guess that gave the cancer time to rebound and the treatments were less effective. We still had hope, though, that she could beat this. Six months later, I lost that job. I was devastated. She needed insurance. Treatment costs were beyond our ability to pay. When I couldn't find work right away, we returned to Michigan. Again, there was a pause in treatment. She finally got need-based state insurance. However, all those interruptions in treatment, I believe, is the reason she is dying." We sat in silence, honoring the pain in his heart.

"Thank-you so much for taking her in. I don't even have a home for her to die in." It was too much. He broke down sobbing.

"You have suffered a lot of setbacks. That's hard," I tried to comfort him. "You did the best you could. There are so many things we don't understand in life. Despite everything, let me assure you that God is in control and that He loves both of you."

Again, we sat in silence. "I don't know that we really believe in God. How could He let all these bad things happen when I tried so hard?" His shattered heart found utterance.

"Sin is behind all the bad things and sicknesses in life. God's love is behind all the good things. He loves you. He has provided this home for you in this difficult time." I let the thought sink in.

"I don't know. I'll have to think about that." Quietly he walked out and left for the evening.

Cheryl suffered a lot of pain. We tried to keep her comfortable, but beyond the physical pain lay spiritual pain. God had surely brought her to Hospice House for a reason.

The Grateful Heart

"Cheryl had a hard night with a lot of pain," the night shift reported one morning. "I think she sees something different about us though. She started asking questions about why we do what we do."

"What will happen to me when I die?" she asked me during her morning care. I shared with her God's plan of salvation and the choice available to her to receive this free gift. She was ready for that heart peace and received the gift with great joy amidst her suffering.

Her husband, seeing her peace and joy, also believed and was saved. Not many days hence, Cheryl went to be with her new-found Lord.

"I feel so bad I couldn't have helped her more. I am so grateful for the spiritual peace we both found here. You were right, every good thing is from God. Thank you for being here for us." With that he followed the stretcher and the funeral home staff out the door.

Four months later, Ralph returned to Hospice House. This time with a gift. A gift of thanksgiving. Four hundred dollars!

"I can't take this from you, you are so poor!" I said as I tried to return the money to him. "God will meet the needs of the Hospice House."

"No, no, please take it! I worked hard to get it for you. I simply must give something for all you and God did for us." He pressed me so hard that I finally felt God must be in it and took his gift. The gift of a grateful heart given to thank a gracious God and a ministry of mercy.

As he walked away, I cried tears of thanksgiving and prayed God to bless him for his sacrificial gift. Like the ten lepers Jesus healed, only one returned with a thankful heart. How often people take for granted the gifts and sacrifices made for them; not considering the cost to the giver nor the expense of the ministry. Nor do they express gratitude for the greater sacrifice Jesus made for their eternal redemption. Oh, that everyone would receive His gifts with thanksgiving. The gift of salvation, the gift to live a full and blessed life, and the gift to participate in ministries God uses to help you. Miserliness denies one the blessing of participation. "But this I say, He that soweth sparingly shall reap also sparingly; and he which soweth bountifully shall reap also bountifully. every man according as he purposeth in his heart, so let him give; not grudgingly, or of necessity: for God loveth a cheerful giver" (II Corinthians 9:6-7).

> "It is a good thing to give thanks unto the Lord, and to sing praises unto thy name, O most High" (Psalm 92:1).

Chapter 30
THE EXAMPLE

"Be thou an example of the believers" (I Timothy 4:12).

"I wonder what God wants me to do here?" queried Sandra as they wheeled the stretcher to her room at Hospice House. She gazed intently as if to memorize her surroundings before she arrived in the bed where she would rest until Jesus came for her.

"I was a Sunday School teacher before I got sick. I loved teaching little children about Jesus," she reminisced. "Now I believe God has a job for me to do here. I know I will be in heaven soon and I want to make each day count for the kingdom!" She exclaimed. Her ebony smile contrasted with her sparkling white teeth.

Hospice House buzzed with activity. Every bed was occupied and many of those patients had many families and friends who visited. Many visited Sandy as well. She could not get out of bed, but she could hear all that was going on. And she could pray. She prayed sometimes quietly and other times she would call someone into her room to pray with them.

"I can't live without my mom." The twenty-Ish young man sobbed in the privacy of Sandy's room.

"Jesus loves you and wants to walk this journey with you. Do you and your mom love Jesus?" she asked. He did not know what she meant. She opened the Bible lying beside her in the bed and showed him God's plan, not only for him, but also for his mom and his whole family. God moved and he tasted to see that the Lord was good. Then he took the pleasant fruit and shared it with his dying mom.

As the Lord lead her, Sandra's high soprano voice rang out beautiful hymns of praise. The Spirit of God often descended like a soft, warm blanket wrapping His love around each one in the house. Strangers to God and to Hospice House remarked that they felt the presence of God when they entered the door. She lived out the scripture,"Be filled with the Spirit; speaking to yourselves in psalms and hymns and spiritual songs, singing and making melody in your heart to the Lord. Giving thanks always for all things unto God and the Father in the name of our Lord Jesus Christ" (Ephesians 5:18b-20).

"Come talk to me," she beckoned an innocent bystander. "What is your name? Who are you visiting?" And thus, she engaged strangers to visit with her. Perhaps they needed comfort or a listening ear. She had time. God placed her here for such a time as this.

"I am so thankful God brought me here. I have had such a wonderful time ministering to people," she whispered to me one day as strength waned from her diseased body. It was hard to realize that she was really dying because she had seemed so full of life. However, on this day there was no doubt.

Soon, Sandra's last task on earth was done. Although Jesus called her home, her influence continues to inspire. The little lady with the ebony skin, the bright smile, and the rejoicing spirit cannot be forgotten. She left an example of the believers to run the race set before them – to the end.

Seems now, as I stand beside the brick that memorializes her time at the Hospice House, I can hear her singing and urging us on from that great cloud of witnesses. She cheers us on through our grief and pain. She encourages us to lengthen our stride as we run this final leg of our race; beckoning us to embrace one more sinner as we run along the way; lift up one more fallen one in our path and together "press toward the mark for the prize of the high calling of God in Christ Jesus" (Philippians 3:14).

May we rejoice with Sandra and all those who have blazed the trail before us and confidently assert with them, "I have fought the good fight,

I have finished my course, I have kept the faith: Henceforth there is laid up for me a crown of righteousness, which the Lord, the righteous judge, shall give me at that day; and not to me only, but unto all them that love His appearing" (II Timothy 4:7-8).

" Finally, beloved," she calls back to us to remember: "Behold the tabernacle of God is with men, and He will dwell with them, and they shall be His people, and God Himself shall be with them and be their God. And God shall wipe away all tears from their eyes; and there shall be no more death, neither sorrow, nor crying, neither shall there be any more pain: for the former things are passed away (Revelation 21:3-4).

"Forget not His Word," she urges: "And, behold, I come quickly; and my reward is with me, to give to every man according as his work shall be. I am Alpha and Omega, the beginning and the end, the first and the last" (Revelation 22:12-13).

"Surely, I come quickly" (Revelation 22:20b).

Conclusion
THE STEWARDSHIP OF GRIEF AND PAIN

"Moreover it is required in stewards, that a man be found faithful" (I Corinthians 4:2).

Portraits of Grace paints word pictures of the grace of God available to any who seek Him. The Comforter, the Holy Spirit, companions us on our journey through grief and pain. His Word is the anchor of our soul.

When a loved one leaves this earthly realm, it may strike us like a massive surgery. An 'amputation' that leaves a deep wound in our heart and life. The initial shock of loss fogs our minds, forbidding us to think clearly or to make wise decisions. Darkness shuts out the light of God's presence, causing us to feel alone or perhaps abandoned. Depression, guilt, anger and a multitude of other emotions attempt to sink our ship of faith. The storms of life rage and block our view of a safe harbor.

Our tears are a language God understands. When there are no more tears, the Comforter translates the deep ache in our heart to the Father. Jesus knows our deep pain. He is present. He grieves with us. Jesus wept at the grave of Lazarus. He wept over Jerusalem. He wept and sweat great drops of blood in the Garden of Gethsemane. He gave us promises to hold onto in the darkness. "Fear thou not, for I am with thee, be not dismayed for I am thy God: I will strengthen thee, yea, I will help thee: yea, I will uphold thee with the right hand of My righteousness" (Isaiah 41:10). "He shall cover thee with His feathers, and under His wings shalt thou trust: His truth shall be thy shield and buckler" (Psalm 91:4).

Every grief, every loss, God can redeem to bring hope and healing to other hurting souls. Jesus came to earth to identify with us, to show us He truly understands our humanity for He, too, was fully human. He experienced life with all its sorrow, pain and grief. He directs our path through suffering. Death came because of sin. Hope comes because of Jesus. Jesus takes the dark strokes of pain and loss, then paints His tapestry with bright colors of love and joy to create a beautiful portrait of our walk through the valley of the shadow of death with Him. The brightness of God's glory shines best as it reflects off our surrendered pain.

The stewardship of pain redefines hope. In the midst of the darkest storm, Job declared his longing for a sense of God's presence. "Behold, I go forward, and He is not there; and backward, but I cannot perceive Him. On the left hand, where He doth work, but I cannot behold Him: on the right hand, that I cannot see him. But He knows the way that I take: when He hath tried me, I shall come forth as gold" (Job 23:8-10). Job suffered multiple layers of loss in a single day. His friends, who came to comfort him, utterly failed. They believed Job must have committed grievous sin for God to punish him so harshly. Still, Job held steadfast to his faith and hope in God, in spite of the distress those denouncements caused him. In the midst of the storm, when darkness veiled God's face, hope redefined found a secure foundation in what Job knew to be the character of God. Job learned God's attributes from a lifetime of fellowship with his Creator. Though he couldn't fathom a reason for his pain and grief, he knew the very character of God to be love. He knew he could depend on God's faithfulness and mercy. He knew God to be holy and perfect. He knew God could not make a mistake. He knew he could trust God. (God also knew that He could trust Job!) His redefined hope longed for restored fellowship with God.

His heart cry echoed the cry of the psalmist, "In God is my salvation and my glory; the rock of my strength, and my refuge is in God. Trust in Him at all times; Ye people, pour out your heart before Him. God is a refuge for us" (Psalm 62:7-8).

God taught me more than I ever wanted to know about grief and pain when He welcomed my beloved husband to Heaven. Many months went by, possibly a year, before I could read the Bible. I listened to the Bible on my phone app by the hour; yet without comprehending what it said. Just listening, however, soothed my bleeding heart.

Fifteen months of grief and pain found expression when I penned these words:

> *Grief knocked on my door one day, I didn't know what to say.*
> *We truly never met before; I didn't know what was in store.*
> *The meaning of 'weep with those who weep',*
> *Was a command I never knew how to keep.*
> *I didn't know the depth of pain*
> *The loss of half of me could drain.*
> *I didn't know tears would forever flow.*
> *That sorrow would hold a death grip on my soul.*

Ten years now have passed. In the depth of my pain and despair, Jesus redeemed my grief as He ministered through my brokenness to wrap arms of love around those in my care at Hospice House. I understood the pain of loss as I never had before. I learned how to 'weep with those who weep.'

The agonizing cries of the bereaved soul plead not to bear a still-birth, but rather to give birth to a redefined hope, a new vision of walking with Jesus.

Stewardship surrenders our pain and sorrow to Jesus, the Man of sorrows, who is the Lord of grief.

Grief proved a difficult journey for me. Perhaps it was complicated by the fact that I dealt with the pain and grief of so many patients and families every day. I felt like I had totally failed to let the Light of Jesus shine through my deepest pain. One day, my Comforter spoke to me through this verse:

"Now unto Him that is able to keep you from falling, and to present you faultless before the presence of His glory WITH EXCEEDING GREAT JOY, to the only wise God our Savior, be glory and majesty, dominion and power, both now and forever. Amen" (Jude 24-25).

He kept and keeps me from falling. To think, in spite of all my doubts and fears and failures, He will present me faultless before the presence of His glory! And He will do it with <u>exceeding great joy</u>! Such love!

That it might be all of God!

ACKNOWLEDGMENTS

All scripture references are from the King James Bible.

Lori Downs provided skillful editing and much encouragement with the manuscript.

Janae Voss taught me computer skills, assisted in the edit and lifted my spirits when I felt defeated.

My daughter, Lisa Michelle Sherrard, guided me from writing nurses notes to painting pictures with words. She was most involved in chapters 1 and 5. I handed her about 10 pages of the first draft for chapter five, reflecting more pain than I knew I carried, and said, "Find the message that brings praise to God. What I have written only magnifies my pain." She searched through the rubble of the destruction of my misguided spiritual foundation and discovered the 'golden brick'. The golden brick I needed. The anchor.

Rachel McCarty for the final fine tune edit and prayers of support.

My sisters, Marilyn Robeson and Katherine Johnson, for reading, editing and encouraging me on this journey.

AUTHOR BIOGRAPHY

Janet Sherrard has lived in Shiawassee County, Michigan most of her life. Redeemed at the age of fifteen, God then called her to be a nurse. In spite of her life challenges, God made a way for His will to be done. She graduated from Hurley School of Nursing in 1970. Her nursing career provided experience in every field of nursing except maternity and psychiatry. The last thirty years of her career, her broad base of hospital experience transferred to the Home Health/Hospice field. She was instrumental in the formation of a non-profit hospice house in her community which continues under new leadership.

Stephanie Judd came to work at the Hospice House and soon discovered a soul-mate and sister in Christ. Though having markedly different backgrounds, unity in Christ bonded them together, enriching the ministry of Hospice House. Stephanie participated in many blessings God bestowed on the House. God also blessed her with communication skills and an eye for detail. Gifts she generously used to prepare the manuscript, find every error in jot and tittle, and make it easy to read and understand. She also interjected wisdom, insight and encouragement from the inception to the finalization of the manuscript.